The Genealogy of Jesus Christ

*Evangelistic Sermons
on the Covenant
from Matthew 1:1*

John Sungchul Hong

EMETH PRESS
www.emethpress.com

The Genealogy of Jesus Christ,
Evangelistic Sermons on the Covenant from Matthew 1:1

Copyright © 2010 John Sungchul Hong
Printed in the United States of America on acid-free paper

All rights reserved. No part of this book may be reproduced, or stored in a retrieval system or transmitted in any form or by any means, electronic, mechanical, photocopying, recording, scanning or otherwise, except as permitted by the 1976 United States Copyright Act, or with the prior written permission of Emeth Press. Requests for permission should be addressed to: Emeth Press, P. O. Box 23961, Lexington, KY 40523-3961. http://www.emethpress.com.

Library of Congress Cataloging-in-Publication Data

Hong, Sung Chul.
 The genealogy of Jesus Christ : evangelistic sermons on the covenant from Matthew 1:1 /John Sungchul Hong.
   p. cm.
 ISBN 978-1-60947-006-7 (alk. paper)
 1. Jesus Christ--Genealogy--Sermons. 2. Evangelistic sermons. 3. Bible. N.T. Matthew I,1--Sermons. I. Title.
 BT314.H66 2010
 226.2'06--dc22   2010027961

Front cover is a digital copy of Hans Baldung, known as Hans Baldung Grien/Grün (c. 1480–1545), a German Renaissance artist. Public domain. Source: http://www.ibiblio.org/wm/paint/auth/baldung/

Contents

Preface..5

Chapter 1. Genealogy of the Covenant...7

Chapter 2. Atop Mount Moriah..13

Chapter 3. The Kingdom of God and Prayer.................................19

Chapter 4. Sources for the Kingdom of God..................................25

Chapter 5. Life of Faith..31

Chapter 6. From the Least to the Greatest.....................................39

Chapter 7. Precious Human Beings in the Image of God.................47

Chapter 8. The Life of a Nomad..55

Chapter 9. Be Prepared..63

Chapter 10. The Genealogy of Life or Death.................................69

Chapter 11. From Defeat to Victory..77

Chapter 12. God's Person...85

Chapter 13. Melchizedek..91

Chapter 14. God's Mission...97

Chapter 15. Faith, Hope, Love & Life..103

Preface

When I was a sophomore in college, one professor required the class to read a portion of the Bible, including the Gospel of Matthew. Matthew was the most tedious of all the books I had ever read. The first chapter in particular was a meaningless and boring piece. I did not understand why that professor chose Matthew as a required book. At that time I was not a Christian and, in fact was putting down Christians.

While I was a senior, through the witness of Christians I met Jesus Christ as my personal Savior and Lord. Or rather, He met me with His saving grace, though I was a terrible sinner. I was positively transformed in every aspect of my life. I began to understand the meaning of life and I reestablished my purpose for living. I also realized a new freedom: freedom from a very self-centered life, and as a result, I began to enjoy a community-centered life.

But another change was that suddenly humanistic literature and secular knowledge did not attract me. Instead, the Word of God became central to my life. The Word was so wonderful that I read it over and over again. Sometimes the Word of God challenged me so powerfully that I had to repent of sins and corruption, and some other times, I was overwhelmed with joyful tears. After knowing Jesus two years I committed my entire life to Christ and to the Word of God.

While meditating on the Bible, I was gripped by Matthew I. I was excited with it, realizing the content of the chapter was related to many parts of the Old Testament. In the process, I began to understand Matthew 1:1: "The genealogy of Jesus Christ, son of David and son of Abraham." As I was contemplating the meaning of that one verse, stories of the Old Testament flashed before my eyes, and I was so inspired that I preached on that verse fifteen times. Eventually I converted the sermons into a book in Korean. The book challenged many preachers as well as lay people. Some preachers said that their messages which were inspired by their reading refreshed their congregations. Many of them have urged me to translate the book into English so that English-speaking Christians could be exposed to this new and fresh approach to the Bible. However, I was so busy teaching and writing that I dared not begin such a challenging project.

Then, a group of Korean students studying at Asbury Theological Seminary volunteered to translate the book into English. I agreed for each student to translate one chapter; therefore fifteen students worked on fifteen chapters. Dr. Jeff Hiatt volunteered to edit the entire book and in so doing greatly improved the coherence of the manuscript. Dr. Larry Wood, my guru and colleague, published it. I owe my heart-felt thanks to each one of them, without whom this book could not have been birthed into the English language.

Furthermore, I want to give all the glory to Jesus Christ, Son of Abraham and of David, Who transformed me so powerfully that I was able to preach and later publish these fifteen messages.

John Hong
Asbury Theological Seminary

Chapter 1

Genealogy of the Covenant

"An account of the genealogy of Jesus the Messiah, the son of David, the son of Abraham." (Matthew 1:1, NRSV).

The Promise in Genealogy

The Gospel of Matthew begins with "an account of the genealogy of Jesus the Messiah, the son of David, the son of Abraham." The word, 'genealogy,' means a pedigree or a clan register. Then why does Matthew, the very first book of the New Testament, begin his Gospel with the introduction of the genealogy of Jesus? The answer is a simple one! It is because Matthew wants to introduce Jesus as the Messiah and actually to frame Jesus within the Jewish expectations of a Davidic Messiah who would restore the Kingdom to Abraham's descendents.

In the beginning, God created Adam and Eve in order to establish the kingdom of God. They did not fulfill their role in God's kingdom, however, because of their disobedience. Since then, every human being, imitating Adam's disobedience of usurping God's role in their life and world, committed all kinds of sins. Look at the people of Noah's time, for example. All that they thought and did was filled with evil. Even after God's judgment of the flood, the people who constructed the Tower of Babel were just as bad.

Genealogy of the Covenant in Abraham, David and Jesus

Even though human history is characterized by human disobedience, God still desires to establish His kingdom in the world. Who is the one God selected to reestablish His kingdom? The one whom God chose is Jesus the Messiah. That is why Matthew introduces Jesus as son of David and son of Abraham in the first chapter.

Then, who was Abraham? As a 75 year old man, he made and sold idols. Who was David? David was a shepherd boy who took care of lambs under the hot sun out in the wilderness. Unfortunately, David grew up without enough love and care from his parents or brothers. Who was Jesus Christ? He was born into a poor carpenter's family and inherited his father's job, becoming another carpenter. Furthermore, He was a man who lived during a miserable era in Palestine when His country was under harsh Roman rule.

Why did God allow this man Jesus Christ, a descendent of ordinary insignificant ancestry to reestablish the kingdom of God? It was because of the grace of God. The word, 'grace' means God's special favor extended to undeserving human beings. Yes! It is through the grace that God pours out unconditionally on undeserving people that He reestablishes His kingdom. In other words, God establishes His kingdom in His own way.

There is another reason why God selects these insignificant people, Abraham and David to restore His kingdom. God wants us to know that God Himself establishes His kingdom in his own way. No mere human being can build the kingdom of God. The greatest scholars, or people of purest virtues with limitless fortunes, or the most exciting religious experiences, or even the ones with the deepest biblical knowledge, cannot build God's kingdom on their own. God used Abraham, David, and Jesus as the means by which God establishes His kingdom through His own method of grace.

How, then, did God pour His grace into these three persons, Abraham, David and Jesus? It was through the covenants God made with each of them. Of course, God did not have any obligation to make a covenant with any one of them. Nevertheless, God gave His grace to each of them, and that grace was expressed in His covenant. Therefore, the first verse of the first chapter of the Gospel of Matthew may be called the genealogy of the covenant.

Genealogy of the Covenant with Abraham

In chapter 12 of Genesis, God said to Abraham; "Go from your county and your kindred and your father's house to the land that I will show you" (Gen 12:1, NRSV). As a 75 old man, this order might have been a preposterous demand, because Abraham was asked to give up his home, homeland, and all that he had achieved. However, this command included the promise of a special covenant. If God's command seemed ridiculous, then the promise was astounding. Think about the promise; "I will make of you a great nation, and I will bless you, and make your name great, so that you will be a blessing. I will bless those who bless you and the one who curses you I will curse; and in you all the families of the earth shall be blessed" (Gen 12:2-3, NRSV).

Until that time, Abraham did not even have any children, and most probably, he would not have any children in the future due to his age. According to this promise, however, he would not only have his own son, but he would become the father of a great nation through his son. Of course, this promise included the bigger plan of restoring the kingdom of God. There was nothing for very old Abraham to do with his own ability but to obey, if he wanted to see this promise fulfilled.

Genesis 15 records that God made the covenant with Abraham and that he would have as many descendents as stars in the sky and the land as all these descendents would ever need. Though an unknown old man, Abraham believed the promise, and God gladly rewarded his faith. As a result of that faith, Abraham became not only the father of Israel, but the epitome (father) of all believing people.

In Genesis 22:18, God gave a specific means of how all human beings could receive the blessing through Abraham; "… by your offspring shall all the nations of the earth blessing for themselves…" Who is your offspring? St. Paul provides the answer of this question in Galatians 3:16: "Now the promises were made to Abraham and to his offspring; it does not say, 'And to offspring,' as of many; but it says, 'And to your offspring,' that is, to one person, who is Messiah" (Gal 3:16, NRSV).

When all these words are put together, Jesus Christ was a descendent of Abraham. At the same time, Jesus is both the divine and human means of blessing by which every person could be blessed by God. For this reason, the Gospel of Matthew introduces Jesus Christ as a descendent of Abraham in its introduction. In other words, the genealogy of the covenant which was begun in Abraham is connected to Jesus.

Genealogy of the Covenant with David

From the covenant mentioned through Abraham, we have begun to understand the partial outline of God's kingdom, though not a perfect one. The kingdom should have people or citizens. People of the kingdom of God are the offspring of Abraham. They are composed of all of the people from around the globe, blessed through Jesus Christ. Who are these persons? They are all the people who have faith; those belonging to all ages and countries. In other words, they are all of the Christians of "all nations, tribes, peoples and tongues" (Rev 2:7).

As already mentioned above, besides its people, the kingdom of God also needs a land. God repeatedly gave Abraham the promise of a land (Gen 15:8, 18; 17:8). Nevertheless, more than people and land are needed to have a complete nation. The reason is simple! The kingdom needs to have a ruler over the people and the land. At a key time in the life of Israel, David was chosen to be such a ruler.

The youngest son of Jesse, David was just a shepherd boy who took care of his father's flocks. At the same time, however, he was a devout person who feared God, meditating on His Word day and night (Ps 1:2). David always depended on God for his daily bread. He depended on God, even while he had to fight wild beasts such as lions or wolves that tried to steal his lambs. God raised the shepherd boy, who completely depended on Him, and made him king. During his 40 year reign, David remained a faithful believer who depended on God and listened to his people.

To this humble ruler, God gave His wonderful covenant. Look at this covenant, "I'll choose one of your sons to be king when you reach the end of your life and are buried in the tomb of your ancestors. I'll make him a strong ruler, and no one will be able to take his kingdom away from him. He will be the one to build a temple for me, and I will establish the throne of his kingdom forever....Your house and your kingdom shall be made sure forever before me; your throne shall be established forever" (2 Sam 7:12-13, 16). According to this covenant, it is God who would establish His kingdom, which is eternal and stable, through one of David's sons.

Then, who is he who will reign over this eternal kingdom? Of course, He is Jesus Christ. Jesus Christ, being one with God is the source of blessing, with which He will bless every nation and person in the world. At the same time, however, Jesus is the King of kings and the Lord of lords who will judge every evil power and spirit that is against God (Rev 17:4). Therefore, the genealogy of Jesus Christ is "the genealogy of Jesus Christ, son of Abraham and son of David."

Genealogy of the Covenant in Jesus Christ

God, who made the covenant with Abraham about the people and the land, also made the covenant with David about being the ruler. Now God's kingdom will be achieved when the ruler over the people appears and restores the Promised Land. The Ruler, Jesus Christ, has at long last appeared in human history to fulfill this great cause. Yes, Jesus is son of Abraham and also the son of David. This is because Jesus appeared to fulfill God's covenants with Abraham and David.

How then did Jesus Christ become the eternal Ruler of the kingdom of God? The answer could be found in the scene of the Last Supper that Jesus had with His disciples. "While they were eating, Jesus took a loaf of bread, and after blessing it he broke it, gave it to the disciples, and said, 'Take, eat; this is my body.' Then he took a cup, and after giving thanks he gave it to them, saying, 'Drink from it, all of you; for this is my blood of the covenant, which is poured out for many for the forgiveness of sins" (Mt 26:26-28).

What does this covenant teach us? This covenant teaches how Jesus Christ, the Ruler, would raise His people. Therefore, this is the covenant that Jesus Christ made with His disciples on the night before His crucifixion. According to this covenant, Jesus Christ would purchase the people of God's kingdom with His torn body and shed blood on that cruel cross, because he was also the Son of God.

Since Adam and Eve were separated from God by their disobedience, they lived without God. In other words, they are "the strangers to the covenant of promise" (Eph 2:12). Their legacy left humanity separated from God in need of reunion and a change of heart because of sinful lives of pride and disobedience. As God promised to Abraham (Rom 4:17), however, Jesus Christ shed His blood on the Cross to restore human beings living without any hope to a right relationship with God. The blood, therefore, was the cost to redeem human from their sins. Human beings (sinners) can become the people of God's kingdom only when their sins are forgiven through His blood.

Yes, Jesus Christ shed His blood on the Cross on behalf of the people lost in sin. It is *the blood of the covenant*, which is the method of forgiving human sins. As God made the covenants with Abraham and David, so the blood of covenant of Jesus Christ cleanses the sins of sinful human beings. As a result, they have begun to live the life under the kingship of Jesus Christ. They have become God's people.

Genealogy of the Covenant in Me

"An account of the genealogy of Jesus the Messiah, the son of David, the son of Abraham" (Mt 1:1) is the genealogy of the covenant. Through studying this genealogy of the covenant, we can discover the kingdom of God. Furthermore, we can learn the indispensable mysteries by which the kingdom of God is established. What are the mysteries? First, as insignificant as we may be, if we will obey Him, we will be allowed to play an important role in God's kingdom.

Second, David lived his life depending on God, taking care of a few lambs in the wilderness (1 Sam 17:28). Likewise, if we really depend on God like David did, we can also become significant people, making a great contribution to the work of revealing God's kingdom and His reign. It does not make any difference whether we may live a life of notoriety or obscurity, with or without approval by our family or society. What matters is obeying God.

Thirdly, Jesus Christ sacrificed Himself completely in order to raise the people of God's kingdom. We should live as He lived, as Christians who have become His people through faith in Jesus' sacrifice. In other words, we have to sacrifice ourselves to further the kingdom of God. Above all, we have to sacrifice with a purpose that sinners may be transformed to be the people of God's kingdom.

The ultimate sacrifice will be the proclamation of Jesus Christ and Him crucified. As Jesus Christ sacrificed Himself, shedding His blood for undeserving sinners who were headed toward death and judgment, we must now also sacrifice ourselves to proclaim the gospel to other people to point them to life and transformation. Then, we are playing an important role in the kingdom of God. Through our proclamation, Christ will raise up people for His kingdom.

Chapter 2

Atop Mount Moriah

"An account of the genealogy of Jesus the Messiah, the son of David, the son of Abraham." (Matthew 1:1, NRSV).

We have already discussed God's grace in the previous chapter from Matthew 1:1. We examined how Jesus Christ is a descendent of Abraham, and a descendent of David. Moreover, we noted how the kingdom of God is revealed through the people of God. Remember how God called Abraham and made a covenant with him: "and by your descendants shall all the nations of the earth bless themselves" (Gen. 22:18).

Later, God called David and anointed him as a king with a surprising promise: "I will raise up your offspring after you, who shall come forth from your body, and I will establish his kingdom. He shall build a house for my name, and I will establish the throne of his kingdom forever" (1 Sam 7:12-13). Since Jesus Christ is the fulfillment of that promise, God accepts all people who believe in Jesus through "the blood of promise" to be the people of God.

Now I will approach to the same text from a different vantage point "atop Mount Moriah" to see what the principles that God used to build his kingdom look like from there. Of course, he showed his plan through "Jesus the Messiah, the son of David, the son of Abraham" (Mt 1:1). It was on Mount Moriah that God met these three persons in special ways.

Abraham atop Mount Moriah

Abraham. Moreover, the son's birth was a miracle, because he was born to a mother, who was past her child baring years and had been unable to give birth. The son, Isaac, was like a treasure to Abraham. Therefore, when God talked with Abraham, He called Isaac, "your son, your only son Isaac".

Meanwhile, God surprisingly commanded Abraham to "go to the land of Moriah, and offer him there as a burnt offering on one of the mountains that I shall show you" (Gen 22:2). This command was very cruel considering what a burnt offering was. A burnt offering was to burn up something completely. In other words, Abraham was commanded to burn his son completely. How cruel is that?

By the way, on which mountain did God command Abraham to kill his son? It was on top of Mount Moriah. On Mount Moriah, Abraham was supposed to offer his only son, Isaac, as a burnt offering. Why was it on top of Mount Moriah? Mount Moriah was three days walking distance away (Gen 22:4). Did God test Abraham to see if he would change his mind during the three days journey, or did he intend for Abraham to suffer for the three days?

If God is love, then why did he make Abraham suffer? God had blessed Abraham in many ways and Abraham was ready to pay for all the blessings. However, that was not what God wanted from Abraham. What God desired from Abraham was to build the kingdom of God through Abraham's only and treasured son!

Abraham could have pleaded with God, "Isaac is the fulfillment of your promise. You promised to build a great nation through my son; therefore, you should not require this of me or my son." However, God was not looking for an argument like that, nor did God need advice. What God desired was obedience. Abraham might have sat around a fire those nights looking up at the stars, counting, pondering his theory and debating God's command. In the end, however, there was only one faithful response.

Abraham decided to obey God's command. Why did he decide to obey? It was because Isaac was a gift of grace from God. In other words, Abraham's son really belonged to God. When God commanded to offer his son as a burnt offering, there was no way to accept it emotionally, or to understand it logically, but he acted in faith and accepted it "willfully." On the next day, Abraham set out with Isaac for the three-days-of-death trip. When Isaac was asked to carry the firewood and to walk to the top of the mountain, he asked "where is the lamb for a burnt offering" (Gen 22:7)?

How Abraham's heart must have burned with this question. He carried his human sadness, but followed God's will. What was the result? God gave Isaac, who was completely offered, back to Abraham. Abraham totally gave *himself* up on top of Mount Moriah and won the victory there for himself, Isaac, and all who would likewise act in faith toward God. Finally, Abraham became a building tool of the kingdom of God. In other words, Abraham emptied himself on top of that mountain and became the ancestor of future believers.

David atop Mount Moriah

Second, Mount Moriah played a role in David's life. Since the time David was anointed as king, the Israelite nation spread out in all directions under his reign. However, he began to have problems in the midst of his success. It was because he became proud and did not depend on God. As a result, he became a corrupted and weak person.

1 Chronicles 21 describes one of the occasions when David succumbed to a seduction. The temptation was for him to count the number of Israelites living in the land. It is called a census in our society. According to God's instructions to Moses, when the census was taken "each person should pay a ransom," that is, give a small monetary offering in remembrance of God's delivering them (Ex 30:12-16). However, David ignored God's law and carried out the census with corrupted pride for his own purposes. David, who was originally a humble person, had become arrogant.

What was the result? God sent a plague to David and his country and seventy thousand Israelites died at once. David immediately confessed his sin in front of God with other Israelites:

> "David looked up and saw the angel of the LORD standing between earth and heaven, and in his hand a drawn sword stretched out over Jerusalem. Then David and the elders, clothed in sackcloth, fell on their faces. And David said to God, "Was it not I who gave the command to count the people? It is I who have sinned and done very wickedly. But these sheep, what have they done? Let your hand, I pray, O LORD my God, be against me and against my father's house; but do not let your people be plagued!" (1 Chr 21:16-17)

Though David became blind by looking at his own self-importance, now he returned to a man of humble heart. Since he confessed his sin with humility, God poured out grace to him. God judges us if we do not repent of our sins, but if we do, he also forgives and heals us (1 Jn 1:9). God commanded David that he should erect an altar to the LORD on the threshing floor of Ornan and offer a burnt offering. Following God's command, David purchased Ornan's threshing floor, offered a burnt offering. God forgave him and restored their relationship.

As a result, Mount Moriah became a place of grace and compassion for David. God used such a place for another important purpose, as described in 2 Chronicles 3:1: "Solomon began to build the house of the LORD in Jerusalem on Mount Moriah, where the LORD had appeared to his father David, at the place that David had designated, on the threshing floor of Ornan the Jebusite."

That is the point! Though David committed a sin and was judged, atop Mount Moriah David was forgiven. David deeply experienced his sinfulness, but by God's grace he experienced forgiveness of sin and recovery of a relationship to God that went deeper than the sin had gone. It is exactly as Paul proclaimed: "But God proves his love for us in that while we still were sinners Christ died for us" (Rom 5:8). Like this, David experienced sinfulness and recovery so that he truly became a person of God.

David saw the depth of his sinful nature. More importantly, on top of Mount Moriah, he experienced the "long, wide, deep, and high" love of God that overcomes sin (Eph 3:19). From then on, he finally became a tool to build and spread the kingdom of God because he could understand himself, God, and others through a mountain top view of God's love.

Jesus Christ atop Mount Moriah

Finally, what significance does Mt. Moriah hold in the life of Jesus Christ? As we saw, Solomon's Temple was built on Mount Moriah. Since that time that Mountain has been a spiritually important place, not only to Israelites, but also to other people because it was a special place of worship. That site has been a place where the holy God met sinful people. It has been a place where God's will was prophesized and proclaimed.

Later, after Solomon's Temple was destroyed, King Herod's Temple was placed there. Many people still sought to meet God at the temple. One day, a young rabbi came to the temple, chased away sheep and lambs, and poured out the coins of the money changers and overturned their tables (Jn 2:15). Then, he reprimanded them with these words, "Take these things out of here! Stop making my Father's house a marketplace! It is supposed to be a house of prayer!" (Jn 2:16ff)

Who was this young adult? It was none other than Jesus Christ. He publically proclaimed, "Destroy this temple, and in three days I will raise it up" (Jn 2:19). What did He mean? He meant this: though God had been present in the Temple that humans built, God would no longer be present there in the same way. Jesus was the divine Word become flesh as the person who fully revealed God's presence in the world (John 1:14).

Confirm that truth, Jesus revealed it this way, "But he was speaking of the temple of his body" (Jn 2:21). This means that the fullness of God dwelt within Jesus Christ. In other words, God is in Christ, and Jesus is in God (Jn 14:10). Therefore, someone who met Jesus, consequentially, met God (Jn 14:7-11).

Let us dig deeper into the meaning of "Destroy this temple, and in three days I will raise it up." Jesus died on the cross in order to forgive all sinners who are captured by guilt and who are enslaved to the fear of judgment. After three days, Jesus Christ was raised from death, like Abraham received Isaac back after three days, and the figurative death of his son.

Jesus Christ fulfilled the spiritual lives of Abraham and David. Mount Moriah was one of the most important places for these three figures' spiritual lives. Jesus Christ died on the cross on the hill called Golgotha, the place of the skull, also known formerly as Mt. Moriah. On that Mountain, His body was broken and his blood was spilled out.

Jesus Christ died atop Mount Moriah because of his love for us, to take away our sin and judgment. However, his ministry did not stop there. After three days, He was raised from death to confirm that our sins were forgiven (Rom 4:25). God accepts everyone who repents of their sins and comes in humility to the foot of the cross. By God's transforming work in them, they become the people of the kingdom of God. And he uses them for his kingdom.

I atop Mount Moriah

What can we learn from the lives of Abraham, David, and Jesus Christ who are associated with Mt. Moriah? First, Christians who are going to be used to build and extend the kingdom of God should go through preparation like Abraham did. There are many different ways to reveal to us exactly who we are on the inside. Maybe, like Abraham, we are clinging to a family member rather than God. Maybe we are involved in a wrong relationship, or we have neglected our spiritual life. Maybe our economic situation has consumed our spiritual life. Whatever the problem is God is willing to forgive us and start our spiritual life anew atop the mountain of His love.

A biblical scholar said, "All tests are about the self that each of us considers as the most important, regardless of the causes of the tests." Once selfishness is revealed, the person loses all their pride. The person is ashamed. The solution cannot be found just anywhere by any means. God pours out his grace, however, and urges the person to come to the cross of Christ, and helps the person to overcome the obstacle in the way.

Sometimes a test is necessary to expose evil. On one hand, and indirectly, a test makes us confront the sin within us. On the other hand, and proactively, a test motivates us to be completely obedient Christians. In other words, a test enables us to join in building the kingdom of God proactively.

Are you going through a time of testing right now? If so, please note what the apostle James said: "My brothers and sisters, whenever you face trials of any kind, consider it nothing but joy, because you know that the testing of your faith produces endurance; and let endurance have its full effect, so that you may be mature and complete, lacking in nothing" (Jas 1:2-4).

Second, Christians who are eager to participate in building the kingdom of God should deeply repent of our sinfulness of ourselves and on behalf of those we represent. Further, we should deeply experience God's grace that deals with and solves that sinfulness. Then, we can sincerely depend on God and reach others in Christ's name.

Even David, who was a man after God's own heart, committed the sin of pride. We, who are jars of clay, can also easily commit sins. We should not be seduced by Satan, the roaring lion, who seeks to devour God's people and to hinder us from loving each other. Let us humbly depend on the Lord: "in the same way, you who are younger must accept the authority of the elders. And all of you must clothe yourselves with humility in your dealings with one another, for "God opposes the proud, but gives grace to the humble" (1 Pet 5:5).

Third, Christians who are used to build the kingdom of God should believe in Jesus Christ's death and resurrection. We should be ready to spread the message of Jesus' death and resurrection whether the time is favorable or unfavorable (2 Tim 4:2). Jesus aligned himself with the Father's will, died on the cross on our behalf, and was raised from the dead to bring the full power and love of God to bear on the world in His kingdom. Christians who are used to build the kingdom of God should die to their own selfish desires. Then, we can experience the power of resurrection with Jesus Christ.

Paul, who contributed much for the expansion of the kingdom of God by spreading out the gospel, said it like this, "I die every day!" (1 Cor 15:31). He also confessed, "I have been crucified with Christ" (Gal 2:19). In other words, "I experience the power of the resurrection everyday" So that "we might walk in newness of life!" (Rom 6:4)

Chapter 3

The Kingdom of God and Prayer

"An account of the genealogy of Jesus the Messiah, the son of David, the son of Abraham." (Matthew 1:1, NRSV).

So far we have considered the themes, "genealogy of covenant" and "on Mount Moriah," through the verse, "an account of the genealogy of Jesus Christ the son of David, the son of Abraham," relating to building up the kingdom of God. Now we turn to the subject, "The Kingdom of God and Prayer." We are about to explore how "prayer" is really a crucial, indispensable factor for building the Kingdom of God. Thereupon, we hope to go through God's graceful presence, connecting with the prayers of Abraham, David, and our Lord Jesus Christ.

Abraham was a man of prayer. King David also was a man of prayer, and we can find prayer in the climax of the life of Jesus Christ. However, if we look deeply into their prayers the emphasis of each has some variation. Abraham interceded to God for his nephew, Lot, who was facing judgment and ruin. King David, on the contrary, petitioned for his own problem. Jesus Christ was praying, embracing his disciples into his deep heart. Each prayer of these three figures can be models for the man who is willing to contribute something to the work of God's Kingdom. Now, we are going to flesh out the models of prayer, seeing the prayer of these three figures.

Abraham, the Kingdom of God and Prayer

First, consider the prayer of Abraham. The Scripture describes Abraham as God's "soul-mate," that is, a very close friend (2 Chr 20:7; Jas 2:23, Is 41:8). How close to God was Abraham? God and Abraham were so close that they shared secrets with each other. Under the intimate relationship, on a certain day God came to Abraham to let him know a special secret. What was the secret? It's recorded in Genesis 18:17- 21: Then the LORD said, "Shall I hide from Abraham what I am about to do? Abraham will surely become a great and powerful nation, and all nations on earth will be blessed through him. For I have chosen him, so that he will direct his children and his household after him to keep the way of the LORD by doing what is right and just, so that the LORD will bring about for Abraham what he has promised him." Then the LORD said, "The outcry against Sodom and Gomorrah is so great and their sin so grievous that I will go down and see if what they have done is as bad as the outcry that has reached me. If not, I will know."

From these verses, we can discover the next three things: First, the Lord God said that He can never ever hide from Abraham, His friend, what He is about to do. The phrase implies that, if He hid something, God would not be a genuine friend (v 17). Second, the Lord God affirmed the covenant with Abraham again (vv 18-19). Third, the Lord God referred to his decision to Abraham that He would not leave the sin and evil of Sodom and Gomorrah unsettled (20-21).

How did Abraham respond to this frightening revelation? He could be impressed with the fact God let him be aware of God's will. He could make an effort to receive more profound revelation, boasting about it and being thankful for it. Furthermore, Abraham could be grateful, with tears in his eyes, for the promise of great blessing on himself. However, it was not due to the greatness of Abraham. He did not overlook the judgment coming upon Sodom and Gomorrah due to the promised blessing upon himself. His heart and spirit was filled with sympathy and compassion for Sodom and Gomorrah who were confronted by God's judgment.

The sympathy did not end with cheap tears or with empty words. Coming to the Lord God, Abraham started interceding, laying down his own life. He began like this: "Will you sweep away the righteous with the wicked (v 23)?" This is an audacious question based upon the word of God, because God can never destroy the righteous. Abraham was not being daring. He was being as humble as he knew how. Let us hear his humility, "Now that I have been so bold as to speak to the Lord, though I am nothing but dust and ashes…" (v 27). Absolutely right! Abraham never demanded anything based on privilege, while coming to the Lord God. God, however, heard Abraham's humble petition, recognizing the fact that he was a creature like dust and a sinner.

Abraham also prayed without ceasing. Hear his prayer, "What if there are fifty righteous people in the city?" (v 24). He petitioned like that even six times. Forty five, forty, thirty, and twenty righteous people in there…

Abraham lastly went down to ten. "What if only ten can be found there?" (v 32). All of his persevering pleadings brought positive answers from the Lord God.

For whom did Abraham pray? First, he prayed for the cities of Sodom and Gomorrah, and second, for his nephew, Lot, and his family, living in the city. Then what was the reason Abraham pleaded consistently like that? Was it because Lot was a faithful nephew, or was it because he had kept a good relationship with Lot? Lot was a nephew who left Abraham 10 years before. Then why did Abraham boldly pray for Lot and his family? The reason was very simple. It was because God revealed to Abraham the deep corruption of Sodom and Gomorrah and the corresponding judgment on their sin. God did not directly show his will to the people insensible to God's word and smudged by sin. The reason God revealed His will to Abraham was that he was prepared and able to pray for Sodom and Gomorrah as an intercessor. Immediately as he grasped God's will, Abraham entered unceasing intercession.

Without exception, God works through prayer that relies upon the Word of God. Moreover, persistent desperate prayer, like Abraham's prayer, certainly receives an answer. Abraham's petitions brought forth two fruits. The first was that God's judgment was postponed (Gen 19:15-16). The second was that four souls, Lot and his wife and his two daughters, were saved from that judgment. Abraham became a significant figure representing the model of intercession for magnifying the Kingdom of God as saving his relatives through his prayer.

David, the Kingdom of God and Prayer

Next, let us view the prayer of David. David obtained the noble name, "a man after God's own heart" (Acts 13:22, 1 Sam 13:14). He was a man of humility. He prayed to depend upon God regardless of whether he was weak or strong. Likewise, God took David from being a poor shepherd boy and appointed him as a glorious ruler of His people. After becoming the king, prosperity and honor were opened for seventeen years to him who unceasingly counted on God to pray.

Then, there came a very severe storm into David's life. In 2 Samuel 11, King David was left alone at Jerusalem after sending armies with the Ark of the Covenant into battle. The Ark of the Covenant of God was the symbol of God's presence and guidance. Why did David not participate in the battle? He got lazy. He became arrogant. He started to make a lot of excuses. Avoiding going along with God, David remained behind to rest at Jerusalem. He shunned companionship with God and sought for rest without God.

What was the result? As we know, he committed adultery with Bathsheba. After learning of her pregnancy, he put Uriah, the husband of Bathsheba, to death in order to hide his sin. He violated the sixth commandment, "You shall not murder," in just one moment. He also broke the seventh commandment, "you shall not commit adultery." He broke the eighth, "you shall not steal," as he stole another's wife. He went against the ninth, "you shall not bear false witness against your neighbor." He trespassed against the last commandment, "You shall not covet your neighbor's house; you shall not covet your neighbor's wife or his male servant or his ox or his donkey or anything that belongs to your neighbor." Finally, as he ignored the word of God, he had no regard for God, Himself. Thus, he consequently broke the commandments from the first to the fourth.

Was David happy? Absolutely not! He also lost the joy of the Lord's salvation. He had a guilty conscience in God's presence. Being unsettled in his soul, he confessed, "When I kept silent about my sin, my body wasted away through my groaning all day long. For day and night Thy hand was heavy upon me; my vitality was drained away as with the fever heat of summer" (Ps 32:3-4).

In this manner, as David was in deep suffering and fierce struggling, God sent the prophet Nathan to him: "Why have you despised the word of the Lord by doing evil in His sight?" (2 Sam 12:9) King David, who had all authority, was able to refuse Nathan's charge. He could logically justify his action. He could impute his guilt on Bathsheba, or imprison or kill Nathan.

However, here is the greatness of David. He started to admit and repent of his sin. His very famous prayers of repentance were written in Psalms 32 and 51. He thoroughly confessed and repented of the sins committed in front of God. He confessed the total corruption of his heart. He confessed his fear of losing the presence of the Holy Spirit. When he laid down all his sin, even the hidden things, God forgave him and restored the joy of His salvation.

This was one of the reasons why David was called "a man after God's own heart." Even though he committed many sins, he openly admitted his sin when confronted by God's word. Moreover, he admitted the sin to Nathan as well as to all the people. Otherwise, how could his prayer of repentance be written in the Psalms? David, who experienced the grace of restoration, did not cease at that point. He began to witness God's hand over all of his directions. Only after going through inner purification in his prayer, could David externally proclaim the impact of God's amazing grace. Then he was able to contribute something to the glory of God's kingdom.

Jesus Christ, the Kingdom of God and Prayer

Abraham unceasingly prayed for the salvation of others. David prayed for his own sin. Then, lastly, what did Jesus Christ, the Son of God, pray? His representative prayer emerges in John 17. The prayer can be divided into three parts: 1) prayer for himself (vv 1-8); 2) prayer for his disciples (vv 9-19); 3) prayer for all believers (vv 20-26).

Jesus prayed for the disciples to have Jesus' full joy in themselves (v 13). Of course, it meant a life of faith full of the Holy Spirit. He also prayed "to keep them from the evil one" (v 15), and to "sanctify them in the truth" (v 17). Every aim of the prayer is one reality in three aspects. Only when we are armed by God's word, can we get victory in the battle with the evil one and be filled with joy.

Jesus prayed for all believers who would have faith through his disciples. The content of the prayer can be summed up in one point: all believers are unified by faith. Only when we become one in the love of Christ will the world recognize Jesus and believe in Him. Above all, the task was dependent upon the disciples and the Holy Spirit to lead people in the world to Christ Jesus. Therefore, after praying for the disciples, Jesus prayed for all believers who would receive the gospel via the disciples.

Hear verse 21 to see the prayer: "That they may all be one; even as Thou, Father, art in Me, and I in Thee, that they also may be in Us; that the world may believe that Thou didst send Me." Jesus knew how to expand the Kingdom of God. The moment Christians unite and love one another, unconditionally, the kingdom is enlarged. The union is impossible without the foundation of prayer. Therefore, Jesus prayed for their oneness [union].

"Me," the Kingdom of God and Prayer

What do the prayers of Abraham, David, and Jesus Christ teach us today? Their prayers clearly teach what we should pray and how we can pray for ourselves as well as all Christians who are eager to expand God's Kingdom. There must be miraculous transformation in individuals, families, and churches, who will pray like the models of prayer they presented.

First, we, like Abraham, should intercede to God for the people in the world who do not know God. We need to experience the power of God's word and receive His blessing like Abraham. Don't be satisfied with only God's blessing for yourselves, pray for the salvation of those among our families, our relatives, and our friends, who are rapidly approaching death and eternal judgment without knowing Jesus Christ. We should pray bravely, as well as humbly, and persistently. We should pray concretely, and specifically about the matter. Above all, we should pray with a heart of love and compassion. We should pray with tears. When was the last time we prayed for a family member, a relative, a friend, or the world with the tears of God in our eyes?

God might not speak to them directly, because there exists a great gulf between God and them (Isa 59:1-2). They disregard the existence of God and have no sense of the love of God. They have no fear of the judgment of God, and live in the midst of sin. They will live a life surrounded by sin tomorrow, just like today. In this way, God is calling us to praying with urgency for them.

Second, we should not just intercede for the salvation of others like Abraham, but prostrate ourselves like David did for inner holiness. Victory over sin and temptation comes through total reliance on the Holy Spirit working in our life. We should tenaciously pray for our own faith. When we confront any temptation, it is time to pray. It is time to pray in repentance when we fall into a sin. Only when we are purified, can we participate in the growth of God's kingdom.

The reason is very simple! God does not use Christians contaminated by sin. God will not hear their prayer. Once David confessed, "If I regard wickedness in my heart, the Lord will not hear" (Ps 66:18). God cannot go along with those who hold sin in their minds. We should humbly repent in order to work out the problem of sin. Coming to the cross, we are purified through the blood of Jesus, so that we can be involved in the proclamation of the Kingdom of God.

Third, we should intercede for one another like Jesus did. We must pray for each other, for protection from the evil one, for holiness through the word of God, and for a life full of joy. More than anything else, all Christians must pray for unity in love. If there is any reason we cannot be one, it is because of me, myself! If there is one who can neither love someone nor be in union due to a certain condition, the self must be the reason for the failure of oneness. Only when we are one in the love of Jesus Christ, can people see Jesus and believe in Him. In this circle, God's kingdom is magnified.

Our church should be a church continuously praying for these three things. In a small group meeting, in men's and women's evangelizing teams, in young adult gatherings, and during the regular Lord's day service, we should pray for (1) the salvation of the unbelievers, (2) one's own holiness, and (3) for unity with one another. Only when the church prays like this can it bear good fruit for the growth of God's kingdom.

Chapter 4

Sources for the Kingdom of God

"An account of the genealogy of Jesus the Messiah, the son of David, the son of Abraham" (Matthew 1:1, NRSV).

We are beginning to understand why the New Testament starts with "the genealogy of Jesus Christ the son of David, the son of Abraham." The construction and expansion of the kingdom of God are accomplished by the principles visible through the lives of these three figures: Abraham, David, and Jesus Christ. The Lord's grace as seen through them reveals what God used for the expansion of the kingdom of God.

The kingdom of God consists of those who are reborn through repentance and faith. They share their faith, lives, and hope within a community of faith called the church. God cultivates His kingdom by reigning in the believers. The kingdom of God communicated through the church is not realized with an empty hand. There is a source that is provided through those in whom God reigns.

The Kingdom of God in Abraham

What kind of source did the father of faith, Abraham, provide to us? To discern it, let us look at the second half of Genesis 14:20: "…Then Abram gave him a tenth of everything." The setting for this text is that the allies of four countries made war against Sodom and Gomorrah. The four countries were Shinar, Ellasar, Elam, and Goiim (Gen 14:1). The allies defeated Sodom and Gomorrah. They took all the property of those places and carried off Abram's nephew Lot, as well (Gen 14:11-12).

When Abram heard this news, he gathered a few soldiers whom he trained at his house. At midnight, he raided the place where his nephew Lot, his family, and property were held captive and rescued them. On the way back, he met Melchizedek, king of Salem and priest of the God Most High. Melchizedek did three things for Abram. First, he gave Abram bread and wine (Gen 14:18). Second, he blessed Abram (Gen 14:19). Finally, he declared that Abram won the battle because of God's help (Gen 14:20).

Abram could easily agree that without God's help, it was impossible not only to defeat the allies of four countries, but to recover everything that was stolen, including his nephew. He immediately gave Melchizedek a tenth of the things that he brought back. As a result, he became known as the father of faith, who left an eternal example to his descendents, by offering, for the first time in the Bible, a tithe of his income.

The tithe that Abram offered is an act that points to the fact that God is the provider of all blessings and property. Then why did Abram offer the tithe? How did Melchizedek use the tenth? In order to answer this, we need to refer to Moses' teachings.

First, a tenth was used for living expense of God's people who served in the tabernacle, like Levites and priests (Num 18:21~24). Second, the tenth was used for the cost related to worship in the tabernacle (Deut 14:22~23). It was also needed in managing and maintaining the tabernacle. Third, it was used for those who need financial help. For example, the needy as well as the people who are devoted to missionary work enter into this category (Deut 28~29). The Kingdom of God was expanded by the tithe's being used in this way.

The Kingdom of God in David

David was a person who always had a deep love for God and wanted to build a temple for God as a place of meeting with the Israelites. Not only this, but he hoped that God would reveal His will and bless His people in the temple. However, he was not allowed to do this because he killed so many people. Instead, his son Solomon built the temple.

When the temple was finally completed, God came upon the temple and His glory filled the temple with fire and smoke (2 Chr 7:1). After that, the news that God blessed the Israelite people spread over the world. As a result, people came from various distant places not only to meet God, but also to see how God blessed the Israelite people. They saw what God did. Consequently, the kingdom of God was being expanded.

Although Solomon built the temple, David had already prepared for it. He longed for the temple. Because of his earnest desire, he first offered three thousand talents of gold and seven thousand talents of silver (1 Chr 29:4). This is an absurd sum that corresponds approximately to $120,000,000 in the present time. Then he says, "in my devotion to the temple of my God I now give my personal treasures of gold and silver for the temple of my God" (1 Chr 29:3).

And David asked his people, "Now, who is willing to consecrate himself today to the LORD?" (1 Chr 29:5). At this question, all the people including the leaders joyfully offered gifts for the temple. They offered a lot of treasure, including five thousand talents of gold, eighteen thousand talents of bronze, and a hundred thousand talents of iron (1 Chr 29:7~8). This is an enormous fund, which is difficult to calculate its value. We see the temple of God was established with what David and his people offered joyfully and boldly.

The Kingdom of God in Jesus Christ

For the construction of the kingdom of God, Abraham offered a tithe, and David offered many talents of gold. Then, what did Jesus Christ offer? He gave everything. He laid aside the glory of heaven for the kingdom of God. He, the Creator of the world, threw away the glory of the world. Satan tested him by showing him all the countries of the world and its glory, but Jesus Christ rejected Satan's way. He rather said: "Foxes have holes and birds of the air have nests, but the Son of Man has no place to lay his head" (Lk 9:58).

Is that all? No! Jesus Christ gave up the most precious thing--himself! This is how economics in the kingdom of God works: "I tell you the truth, unless a kernel of wheat falls to the ground and dies, it remains only a single seed. But if it dies, it produces many seeds. The man who loves his life will lose it, while the man who hates his life in this world will keep it for eternal life" (Jn 12:24~25).

"Many seeds" from this passage means those who receive Jesus Christ through repentance and faith. They compose the kingdom of God. Jesus Christ proclaimed the kingdom of God in his public ministry, "Repent, for the kingdom of heaven is near" (Mt 4:17). Then how does he build the kingdom of God? It is through his death. For this reason, he had to die as a kernel of wheat.

With his extremely cruel and sad death before him, Jesus Christ prayed: "My Father, if it is possible, may this cup be taken from me!" (Mt 26:39). This cup of death, cup of blood, cup of sin--the price of human beings—was extremely cruel. However, he went on pray for the building of the kingdom of God: "Yet not as I will, but as you will!" (Mt 26:39)

Jesus Christ came to earth to bring the kingdom of God on earth. For this purpose, he lived his short life, and gave his body and blood as an offering of sacrifice (Heb 9:12). That is the very way to build the Kingdom of God. He did this so that since then, whoever follows Jesus Christ, who died on the cross, can become the people of the kingdom of God.

The Kingdom of God in Me

We have succinctly touched on what sources Abraham, David, and Jesus Christ used for building the kingdom of God. Abraham offered a tithe, David offered his treasure, and Jesus Christ offered his life. Then, what does this lesson teach us? We can get the following three lessons.

First, it is important to tithe. The tithe is essential for the expansion of the kingdom of God. God saved us from sin and judgment. God allowed us to live in a free country, not in a country where there is no freedom. God gave us health and friends. God gave us home and church. All of these are gifts from God. Because these all belong to God, they must be used as He wants.

R. T. Kendall, a pastor of Westminster Chapel in Great Britain, teaches about a perfect tithe: "Lay people must offer a tithe to the church from which it provides spiritual bread." It is so as long as the church does not use the offering unbiblically. The offering must be used for the salaries for church employees, and the costs related to worship and outreach, that is, missions and development.

The Bible clearly teaches, "A tithe of everything from the land, whether grain from the soil or fruit from the trees, belongs to the LORD; it is holy to the LORD" (Lev 27:30). Jesus says, "Woe to you, teachers of the law and Pharisees, you hypocrites! You give a tenth of your spices--mint, dill and cummin. But you have neglected the more important matters of the law--justice, mercy and faithfulness. You should have practiced the latter, without neglecting the former." (Mt 23:23).

Yes! We should not discard personal faith, nor should we abolish the habit of the tithe. God promises that if we offer a tithe, God is pleased to bless us. Listen to the Word of promise, "Bring the whole tithe into the storehouse, that there may be food in my house. Test me in this," says the LORD Almighty, "and see if I will not throw open the floodgates of heaven and pour out so much blessing that you will not have room enough for it" (Mal 3:10).

A biblical scholar once said, "All saved people offer a tithe. God pays back to those who voluntarily offer to God. God takes it back from those who do not follow His method." This means that God necessarily takes off the tithe. Such people not only "are dispossessed," but also there is none of the guidance, joy, and shalom that He gives. All saved people participate in the expansion of the kingdom of God by offering a tithe to God.

Second, as David prepared for building a temple by offering his treasure, we Christians should use our treasures for the expansion of the kingdom of God by offering them back to God. Although the talent that David offered was money, there are various meanings of talent in the New Testament (Mt 25:14 ff). God gave all Christians different talents. Whatever they are, they are given for use in the kingdom of God.

In the New Testament, Jesus tells about a person who misused his talent by covering it with a piece of cloth and hiding it in the ground instead of putting it to work (Mt 25:25, Lk 19:20). The ground symbolizes this world, and cloth symbolizes the self. This means we should not to use the talent that God gave us in worldly ways or selfishly. God took it away from the selfish, unfaithful person and gave it to a faithful one (Mt 25:28). This application includes both the present and future judgment. In the present, those who use their talents for the kingdom of God are given more opportunities. Therefore, whatever talents that God gives us, we must use them for the kingdom of God with humility and a thankful attitude.

Third, Jesus Christ laid the foundation for the kingdom of God by offering Himself. We should offer ourselves for the task. Our treasure is needed for building the kingdom of God. Our skills are also needed. However, there is something much more important and valuable than they are. It is we ourselves. If we cannot offer ourselves, then how valuable are the few treasures and talents that we offer for the kingdom of God?

The apostle Paul teaches, "And they did not do as we expected, but they gave themselves first to the Lord and then to us in keeping with God's will" (2 Cor 8:5). Why should we offer ourselves for the kingdom of God? First, it is because we are saved by Jesus' blood. That is to say, He delivered us from sin by His blood. Therefore, we are not ours, but Jesus Christ's (1 Cor 6:20).

Second, it is because we are the temples of the Holy Spirit that He dwells in. We should obey as the Holy Spirit commands. Third, somebody shared the gospel with us at his or her expense, and as a result we became people of God. In other words, we all owe the debt of love to somebody else. Fourth, it is because of the future reward given in the kingdom of God. Jesus said, "If anyone would come after me, he must deny himself and take up his cross daily and follow me" (Lk 9:23). Yes, the most important thing for building the kingdom of God is us ourselves. If we offer ourselves as "living sacrifices" (Rom 12:1), then the kingdom of God will be expanded for sure.

Chapter 5

Life of Faith

"An account of the genealogy of Jesus the Messiah, the son of David, the son of Abraham" (Matthew 1:1, NRSV).

The first Sunday worship service of the New Year is a very important service. We are given the opportunity to decide the direction of our spiritual life for the next year. At this important New Year's worship service, today's word will be very appropriate. Why? This verse is the very first message of the New Testament as well as the beginning of the book of Matthew.

One reason that the passage "an account of the genealogy of Jesus Christ the son of David, the son of Abraham" is important is because Abraham is the founding father of the Jews, David is the first king of the Jews, and Jesus is the Savior for all people including the Jews. Each of these three people lived "lives of faith;" thus, they give us direction how to live a new year through faith.

Abraham, David and Jesus give important direction to the church which enters the New Year with preparedness to grow in quality as well as in quantity. The lives of faith of these three people are an important example to churches who want revival.

Why is faith needed? Faith is needed because it is impossible to please God without faith. Let's take a look at the well-known verse of Hebrews 11:6. "And without faith, it is impossible to please God …" Our faith pleases God and is the means by which we can receive His grace. The next question is this: "What is faith?"

The answer to that question is found in Hebrews 11:6. According to this verse, faith has two aspects. "Because anyone who comes to him must believe that he exists and that he rewards those who earnestly seek him." According to this, the first aspect is to believe in the existence of God and the second aspect is to believe that He will meet those who seek Him and believe in His works.

Life of Faith in Abraham

One day God called Abraham at the age of 75. "Leave your country, your people and your father's household" (Gen 12:1). Abraham gave up his former life style, obeyed the word of God, and lived his life as "aliens and strangers," that is, as a pilgrim following God's guidance (Heb 11:13). What made his pilgrimage possible was his faith in God who prepared "a better country" for him (Heb 11:16).

When God called Abraham He also gave him a wonderful promise. He would make Abraham's descendants into a great nation (Gen 12:2). Although Abraham trusted in God's call and his promise, he took it into his own hands and looked for ways to fulfill the promise. Abraham chose to adopt his nephew as his son. For that purpose he brought his nephew, Lot, on his journey, violating God's order to leave your people and your father's household.

God not only fulfills his promises, but he does it through his own ways. For that reason, God had Lot leave Abraham (Gen 13:11). Abraham was a man of faith who left his home following God's call, but he was still a person who tried to do things on his own in his own timing. Otherwise, how could he justify another adoption of Eliezer to bring about God's promise?

God confirmed again his promise, "I will make you a great nation." Let's look at Genesis 15:5, "'Look up at the heavens and count the stars.' Then he said to him, 'So shall your offspring be.'" Abraham believed this huge promise without hesitation. The Bible describes his faith like this, "Abram believed the LORD, and he credited it to him as righteousness" (Gen 15:6).

The term "belief" in this verse is the first word that was used in the Bible to describe faith. Abraham received God's promise and his method with sincerity. His faith was gradually made purer and purer. From then on, no matter what the situation was he did not try to fulfill the promise of God through relatives or adoption. He believed God would fulfill his promise through a true son of Abraham called by God.

Abraham's faith needed to be more refined and developed because he had a son with his Egyptian maidservant, Hagar, and expected the fulfillment of the promise of God through that son (Gen 16:4). However, that was still Abraham's own efforts to fulfill God's promise. Although Ishmael was Abraham's son, Ishmael was not from his wife, Sarah.

Ishmael was a son born by human method outside the promise and will of God.

Finally, after Abraham and Sarah became too old to have a baby, Isaac was born to fulfill the promise of God (Gen 21:1). Abraham was 100 years-old and Sarah was 90 years-old at that time. It was impossible for Sarah to give birth to a son for she was barren, but she had a son anyway by having faith in God the Almighty (Heb 11:11).

Because of these works of God, Abraham's faith was deepened. As a result, Abraham did two things. First, Abraham separated himself from Ishmael, whom he had loved for 13 years (Gen 21:14). Second, Abraham offered his son, Isaac, as a sacrifice on the mountain of Moriah. He believed that God would fulfill his own promise by his own method (Heb 11:17).

Life of Faith in David

When did David show his faith? Several times, however, the faith he had when he fought against Goliath was very special (1 Sam 17). The Israelites and the Philistines were at war. It was decided that the champion from each side would fight, so the Philistines sent Goliath. The leader of the Israelites was King Saul, but the Israelite army lost their desire to fight when they saw Goliath's size and strength. As a fierce fighter, he was very tall like a tree and his weapons were dreadful.

His challenge was clear. "Are you not the servant of Saul? Choose a man and have him come down to me" (1 Sam 17:8). King Saul was astonished and the people trembled at this challenge. Although Saul was a tall and impressive man (1 Sam 9:2) he was seized by dread and fear. Jonathan, his son, who had killed 20 Philistines, was there, but he also could do nothing (1 Sam 14:14). Even the commander of the army, Abner, could not and would not respond to Goliath's challenge (1 Sam 14:50, 26:15).

It was David who appeared on the battlefield at this moment. He did not come as a soldier. He was on an errand to bring food to his brothers on the battlefield. He was just a shepherd boy in charge of his father's flocks of sheep. He heard the challenge of Goliath and he dared to respond to that challenge. Although he was just a small child, he was a man of faith who firmly trusted in God Almighty. Where was David's faith developed, which caused him to respond to the challenge even the commander avoided? It was developed in normal times. David learned and mastered how to trust God while he was shepherding flocks of sheep in the field of Bethlehem. He meditated on God's words day and night

(Ps 1:2), prayed to God (Ps 5:1), and followed God (Ps 23:2). Trusting God, David fought with the lion and the bear (1 Sam 17:37).

Although Saul and the people were terrified of Goliath, David looked at him in the eyes of God. And he decided Goliath was just like a lion or a bear. Although Saul and the people forgot God who led them until now, David remembered God who rescued him from dangers. He did not doubt God who would be with him in this danger.

Eliab, the oldest brother of David, rebuked him (1 Sam 17:28) and even Saul tried to dissuade David from engaging in this battle that seemed impossible for them to win (1 Sam 17:33). Is that all? When he saw David, Goliath cursed and threatened to kill Him (1 Sam 17:43-44), but David, a man of faith, trusted God who is greater than all that is fearful. He declined the coat of armor from Saul, and, without spear or sword, he went to face the giant. He only took his staff and 5 stones. He was convinced to trust God only.

David fought with Goliath with this confession: First, "I come against you in the name of God" (v 45). Second, "God will hand you over to me, and I will cut off you head" (v 46). Third, "As a result, the whole world will know God" (v 46). Fourth, "It is not by sword and spear that the LORD saves" (v 47). Confessing this tremendous faith, David slung the stone; Goliath fell, and there was a great victory for the Israelites that day.

Life of Faith in Jesus Christ

Jesus Christ is God and human at the same time. Therefore, he does not need faith. Rather, he told his followers that it is the works of God to believe in him (Jn 6:29). In other words, it was an indirect announcement that he himself is God. Yes! Jesus Christ is God who had come in human form. That's why he said "Anyone who has seen me has seen the Father" (Jn 14:9).

He was at the same time a human. There had been a great challenge to Jesus, when his friend, Lazarus died. It had been four days. The Israelites thought that the soul of a dead person would leave the body on the third day. Then how could he cause dead Lazarus to live again as late as the fourth day?

Jesus prayed in front of the tomb of Lazarus. When we look at the content of the prayer, we can see that there was great faith in it. "Father, I thank you that you have heard me… But I say this for the benefit of the people standing here, that they may believe that you sent me" (Jn 11:41-42).

Jesus didn't have any doubt about God's ability to answer his prayer. It was a prayer filled with faith from beginning to end, in which any doubt could not be seen. Otherwise, how could he shout in front of the people like this? "Lazarus, come out!" (Jn 11:43). In response to Jesus' call, Lazarus came alive. What a great result of faith!

Jesus prayed and acted with a firm confidence in being answered. There were three works due to Lazarus' coming alive from the dead. First, the word of Jesus was achieved. "I am the resurrection and the life. He who believes in me will live, even though he dies," this word of Jesus was realized (Jn 11:25). Second, believers, especially his disciples, could see the glory of God (Jn 11:40). Third, people came to believe that God sent Jesus to save the world (Jn 11:42).

Life of Faith in Me

Through this verse, we see that Abraham, David and Jesus Christ provided an important principle for the kingdom of God. By faith, Abraham started his pilgrimage. By faith, David won the victory. By faith, Jesus Christ caused the dead man to live. Then, what is the teaching of the faith of these three people? We can find them as follows:

Abraham had faith when he was called, but his faith was not perfect at the start. His faith gradually became mature through using it. He began with a trial and error approach over the promise about having a son. His faith was one with a lot of human interference. However, whenever faith appeared, God worked through these human methods. Of course there was pain. But that kind of pain is like a medical treatment. When there is a wound, it needs antibiotic cream or shots to cure it. That process results in pain, but that pain is the process of treatment and brings even greater healing.

We Christians have both a faith aspect and a doubt aspect at the same time, like Abraham. At first, the doubt aspect tends to win. We think, decide, and behave as we wish regardless of the will of God in the Bible. It might make us feel good for a while, but as time passes we begin to realize it is wrong. We have no peace and we find ourselves reproaching others for the same things we do ourselves.

Christians should want to escape from this contradictory life, but it is not easy for us to acknowledge that our thinking, decisions, and behavior are wrong. It is even more difficult to give them up, than simply to acknowledge them. To do that is often both difficult and painful. To break out of doubt is very hard; thus, many Christians live below their privilege.

When Abraham finally gave up his own methods, God gave him a son like He promised. Likewise, God gives us spiritual children as much as we Christians give up our own methods. That is, he allows the fruit of evangelism. I hope our faith becomes mature like Abraham. Then, through all of us, many people will be led to Jesus Christ.

Second, although David was a shepherd boy, he defeated Goliath by trusting God. How could it be possible? David maintained a deep fellowship with God everyday. He meditated on the words of God day and night, prayed, and experienced the guidance of God. As a result, he could overcome the crisis by trusting God, going to the battle, and singing the praises of the victory.

It is the same for us as Christians. From time to time, we will enter into the spiritual battlefield. For the power of the evil will not leave us alone. Especially, when we try to live the life of faith like Abraham, evil spirits will attack us heavily. As a result, we could tremble and fear as the Israelites did before Goliath. We may have a desire to avoid these spiritual attacks.

For this kind of spiritual warfare, we need to maintain a deep fellowship with God in everyday life as David did. The fight of our Christian lives is finished in the closet. If we read God's words, meditate and pray in our prayer closets, then, we cannot lose that fight. However, if we do not have quiet time with God, we will be defeated in that fight for sure. Therefore, we have to have a "closet hour" everyday. By doing so, we can maintain a year of faith which gives us a victory in our spiritual battle.

Each of us has a Goliath in our lives. One may have a Goliath who hinders his everyday Bible reading. Another may have a Goliath who hinders his faithful prayer. Another may have a Goliath who causes him to be lazy. Another may have a Goliath who makes him disobey the clear will of God. And another may have a Goliath who hinders him from preaching the gospel.

Trusting God Almighty, David confronted Goliath with the name of God. And he fought against Goliath in God's name. At last, he won the victory by the name of God. Likewise, we need to confront Goliath with the mighty name of God. And we also can win whatever our personal Goliath is by the mighty name of God. God the Almighty will give us a huge victory.

Third, Jesus Christ was the God-man, that is, he was God and a human. He was God who did not need to pray. However, Jesus, as a human, prayed to God. It was not a plain prayer but a prayer with faith. As a result, dead Lazarus became alive. His words were achieved literally. There were two works accomplished by the words of Jesus.

First, above, God was glorified. Second, below, a lot of people began to have faith.

It is the same to us, so called little Christs or Christians. We need to believe the words of God without any addition or subtraction and we should pray a prayer of faith according to the words. However, our motives underlying the prayer should be pure. Like Jesus Christ, our prayer should be for the glory of God above and for the faith of others below. In doing so, God will show us a miracle that is impossible to us. He will bring people to life like he did to Lazarus.

Let us Christians live a life of belief for miracles in our individual lives, at home, at school, and at our place of business; driven by our prayer of faith! And further, let our church make miracles. Let's seek a spiritual revival and external growth. A life with miracles is possible through the prayer of faith. God is the only one who makes miracles.

Chapter 6

From the Least to the Greatest

"An account of the genealogy of Jesus the Messiah, the son of David, the son of Abraham" (Matthew 1:1, NRSV).

Have you ever heard of Corrie Ten Boom? She was a common woman who grew up in a normal family in The Netherlands. Her father sold and fixed watches and clocks. This normal girl, Corrie, is known all over the world. Why was she so famous? The reason is the great God in whom that girl and her family believed. However, she did not become famous all of the sudden. It took a long time for her to become famous. She suffered many difficulties in her life.

The people who accept Jesus Christ as their Savior and live according to his will are not "common" people. It is not because *they* are so great, but because the God whom they believe in is the greatest. For this reason, to know about the character of a person, we need to see the faith of the person. If we can see the faith of the family, we can see the morality of the family. The future of the nation also can be projected by the faith that controls the government.

The three figures in this verse had similar experiences. All of them have a degree of fame. Is there any Jew, Christian, or Muslim who does not know the name of Abraham? Of course not. How about David? He also has a high reputation. Jesus' fame is near universal. Even non-believers know the name of Jesus. The amazing fact is that these three people started their lives as normal, common people. Their beginning is not that different from ours. It was even lower than some of our lives. The ends of their lives, however, were remarkable. They became great people. The reason is very simple: it is because of the God they believed in is the Almighty.

Abraham from Obscurity to Exaltation

Abraham was an ancient Babylonian or Chaldean whose nation governed the world that was known to them at that time. Abraham married Sarah and ran his own successful business supplying their household with food, clothing, and some of the comforts of living. In an anecdote, it is said that he made the god of the moon for a living. By this time Abraham was about 75 years old, so, I suppose we could say that he had been moon-lighting for most of his life!

Ancient Babylonia was filled with various kinds of idols and their worshippers. Babylonians especially worshiped the natural phenomenon as idols. For example, they worshiped nature like the sun, moon, stars, fire, etc. Such idolatry was connected to fertility and ritual sexual intercourse. In other words, Babylon worshiped creatures and longed for sexual pleasure instead of worshipping the Creator. The center of idolatry was the well-known Tower of Babel (Gen 11:4).

Abraham's father and grandfather had been idolators. The Bible puts it, "…Long ago your forefathers, including Terah the father of Abraham and Nahor, lived beyond the river and worshiped other gods" (Jos 24:2). Abraham was born and grew up in a family and a society that worshiped various gods.

If Abraham had continued to worship other gods as his ancestors did, and to make idols of the moon god, could he be such an important man in the Bible? Of course not! He might have worshipped other gods, lived an immoral life, and left this world in obscurity. Then his name would have been forgotten forever. Abraham, however, rejected the immoral life, and God exalted him.

Why did he refuse idolatry when it was prevalent at that time? Did he feel that life was empty? Was he sorry that he did not have any children? Did he see through the uselessness of idols made by human hands? Did he recognize the limits of moral decadence? Was he afraid of death? Whatever his reasons were, Abraham finally rejected the idolatry which his ancestors and the community had accepted. Instead, he turned to God the Creator. He daringly left the society which was filled with idolatry, and started to live by depending on God. He had reached a turning point in his life.

Abraham's life was not without troubles, nor was it all rose-colored. He sometimes suffered because of misunderstandings by his relatives (Gen 13:11). He was persecuted by others from time to time (Gen 12:15, 20:2). Sometimes Abraham took matters into his own hands, not following God's leading, and made mistakes (Gen 16:2). Despite these mistakes, however, Abraham never forgot God. Nor did he leave God. He thought of God when he was weak and when he was strong.

What is the result of trusting God? First, Abraham became the physical ancestor of the nation of Israel (Isa 51:2). Israel has a small population compared to other nations, but it is a world leader in the economy, military, and science. Second, he became the ancestor of the Arab Empire that produces oil and has more than three hundred million people. Third, Abraham became the ancestor of all believers who follow Jesus Christ (Gal 3:7). Fourth, his name was mentioned the most in the New Testament except for Moses. Fifth, Jesus Christ, who is the Savior of the world, is called the son of Abraham (Mt 1:1).

What made the humble seventy-five year old Abraham a famous person? He did not *do* anything at all. He did not help the poor, study much, serve well, or offer large offerings. What he did was to turn away from idolatry and followed the living Creator God. The Almighty God whom Abraham followed made Abraham an exalted father of many nations.

David from Anonymity to Celebrity

David was just one of the numerous decedents of Abraham. He was just another grain of sand on the beach. David was born in the small town of Bethlehem in Israel (Mic 5:2). It was like Abraham Lincoln being born into a poor rural family in Kentucky.

What was David's family like? His grandfather, Obed, was born to Boaz and Ruth. This family could have serious problems because Boaz was an Israelite, but Ruth was a Moabite. In the past, Israelites despised people from Moab. Moses proclaimed in his commandments that the offspring of Mohab could not enter the Israel assembly permanently, because the Moab army opposed Israel on the way to the promised land of Canaan from Egypt (Deut 23:3; Num 21:21-24).

David was the youngest son in this faulty family. He felt that his parents loved his brothers more than him and ignored David. David's duty was taking care of sheep out in the fields (1 Sam 16:11). On the other hand, his brothers were leaders and warriors in serving their king and country. David's most honorable work was to deliver food to his brothers who were in the war (1 Sam 17:17).

One day, the prophet Samuel visited this small town of Bethlehem. The elders of the town trembled when they met him and greeted him (1 Sam 16:4). He had a meal with Jesse's family. Samuel visited Jesse's family not only to convey the will of God, but also to choose one of his sons to anoint as the king who would succeed the current reigning Israelite Commander-in-Chief, King Saul. Jesse never even thought to invite David to this important meeting. David was nothing but a lowly shepherd to Jesse.

God gives grace to the humble, and had other plans for this anonymous and overlooked youth. God anointed David, and made him a king of Israel (1 Sam 16:12). He did not become the king right away. He suffered many difficulties and wept bitter tears on several occasions. In jealousy, King Saul tried multiple times to kill David, but David escaped from Saul and eluded him for a long time. David lived in the forest and in the caves. He was almost caught by Saul. Sometimes, he was chased by armies of other countries and suffered from hunger.

Nevertheless, David eventually became king. Moreover, he became the most celebrated king in all Israelite history. He accomplished the great work of uniting all the tribes of Israel. He prepared all the necessary materials so that his son, Solomon, could build a huge and glorious sanctuary to God. His greatest accomplishment was not to be found in his wars or material gifts listed, but in spiritual things.

God uses the prepared bowl. God promised David an everlasting house and throne because he was a dedicated man (2 Sam 7:13). According to his promise, God sent an everlasting throne, Jesus Christ, among the decedents of David. In this reason, Matthew chapter one and verse one calls Jesus Christ as "son of David." There are several quotes in other Gospels that Jesus mentioned by himself. "I am the root and the offspring of David, and the bright morning star" (Rev 22:16).

That is right. How is this possible, that the anonymous David became a man of celebrity status? That is why the God in whom David believed was great. How did David show his faith to God? First, he was faithful in keeping a flock of sheep, believing that God gave him the work of keeping sheep. Even when lions or bears attacked his sheep, David defended the sheep at the risk of his own life. Could any shepherd be more faithful for a sheep than even to risk death?

Second, when he became a king, David ruled the nations faithfully for the glory of God, not for his own glory or benefit. The Bible declares that, "[God] chose David his servant and took him from the sheep pens from tending the sheep he brought him to be the shepherd of his people Jacob, of Israel his inheritance. And David shepherded them with integrity of heart, with skillful hands he led them" (Ps 78:70-72).

Jesus Christ from the Least to the Greatest

Where does Jesus Christ fit in this story? In human sight, there may not be any other person lowlier than Jesus. Why is this? First, look at the time of his birth. His country was destroyed 600 years before he was born. For that long period, the Israelite nation was laid waste by many other nations. At first, Israel was destroyed by Babylon. Then it was conquered by Medo-Persians and by the Grecian empire led by Alexandra the Great. Then, Egypt and Syria devastated it in turn. Finally, while Israel was being trampled by Rome, Jesus Christ was born.

Israel became poorer and poorer after the ravages by many countries. Diseases were prevalent because of poor sanitation throughout the country. Others were dying of starvation (Lk 7:12, 8:49; Jn 11:14). More than this, some people were trapped by the devil. Jesus was born in the dark era when there was no hope in any place: North, South, East or West.

Second, Jesus Christ was born of the Virgin Mary. This was an Immaculate Conception by the Holy Spirit. However, what a humble start of life it was to be born to a very young woman. Mary and Jesus Christ might have lived under the contempt and derision of other people. Jesus Christ had his spiritual father, God, but he did not have a biological father, although Joseph was his legal father.

Third, Jesus is a lowly person because of his place of birthplace. He was not be born in his own hometown, but during a trip, like a refugee. More than this, he was born in a barn, because there was no hospital, no motel, or even a friendly home. If the weather had been harsh, or without the devoted care of Joseph, the legal father, Jesus and Mary both easily could have died.

Fourth, Jesus Christ lived a short life of 33 years and was put to death on a cross. At that time, death on a cross meant the most gruesome and disgraceful death. Before the death on a cross, Jesus' body was already smeared with blood from the hours of torture he endured. In this weak state, they nailed his hands and feet. Moreover, He had bled to death for six hours on a cross. Was there any lowlier person in the human history than this one?

God raised this lowly person, however. How did God raise him so high? First, three days after Jesus died, God raised him. As He was entirely human, He was also entirely divine. As a result, Jesus became the Savior of human beings who cannot escape from a death. All human beings die because they are sinners. Jesus became the Savior, who would remove the bridle of sin and death from those who turn to him.

Fifth, God made Jesus Christ to be worshipped by people. The people who were saved from the bridle of sin and death through Christ's death on a cross and resurrection cannot do any less than worship him. For this reason, Christians gather on Sundays to worship and praise him. We give him our hearts while worshipping. We give him our highest respect and honor. We confess with our lips that He is the Savior who freed us from sin and death.

Finally, God made Jesus "Lord." What does Lord mean? Lord means ruler. In his resurrection, Jesus Christ proved that He ruled over death. For this reason, the people who accepted him as their Savior confess that Jesus Christ is the Lord, because he solved the problem of death. Jesus Christ became our Lord by being obedient to God to the end.

I from the Least to . . . ?

From Abraham, David, and Jesus Christ, we learned about their lowly beginnings and their very humble lives. We also saw that all of them became great persons because of their great relationships to God. The lives of these three persons, Abraham, David, and Jesus Christ, teach us three important lessons.

First, we have to choose to follow God like Abraham did. What does it mean to choose to follow God? It means that Abraham threw away idol worshipping that was prevalent at that time. What on earth does idol mean? Idol means the things that people have made to worship or the center around which they order their lives. Specifically, it means everything that people regard as more important than God is an idol. Everything that disrupts the relationship between God and us is an idol.

To choose God means to throw away those idols. What is more important to us than God is? Is it a reputation? Is it money? Is it family? Is it honor? Abraham even left his hometown and parent's house to follow God. As a result, God made Abraham an important person. It applies to us in the same way. If we follow God in a right way, God will make us a great person, whether we have world-wide fame or not!

Second, we have to be faithful in doing little things like David was faithful even in seemingly trifling work. Even though David was treated contemptuously by family and roughly by his surroundings, he gave his best to a little thing while thinking of God. Finally, he became a great man. This is the principle that follows God's will. God charges a great work to the people who are faithful to a little work. In other words, he makes them that great!

Jesus Christ talked about this principle. "Whoever can be trusted with very little can also be trusted with much, and whoever is dishonest with very little will also be dishonest with much" (Lk 16:10). God is still looking for a person who can be trusted with very little. After finding the person, God prepares him or her through training, and even suffering, to make him or her useful to the kingdom.

Third, the life of Jesus Christ, from the birth to death, can be summarized in a word. The word is *obedience*! The author of Hebrews summarized the life of Jesus Christ as follows: "Although he was a son, he learned obedience from what he suffered and once made perfect, he became the source of eternal salvation for all who obey him" (Heb 5:8-9). As Jesus Christ has lived, we also have to live a life of obedience.

God blesses us upon our obedience. How does He bless us? First, He pours the Holy Spirit on us. God pours the Holy Spirit on those who ask, trust and obey him in order to provide them the ability to obey more (Acts 5:32). The second blessing is by growing beautiful fruits through obedience. For example, God allows the fruit of evangelization as well as the fruit of pleasure when we obey and evangelize. Third, God changes us into the precious people whom others love and trust. This happens because obedience is a virtue that pleases God. If we follow him on the path of obedience, we too will be one of his . . .**greatest**!

Chapter 7

Precious Human Beings in the Image of God

"An account of the genealogy of Jesus the Messiah, the son of David, the son of Abraham" (Matthew 1:1, NRSV).

Human beings were created in God's image. It means human beings are like God. Which part of a human being is similar to God? As we know, we cannot see God with our eyes. God is invisible. So, it means that human beings have a spiritual and inner similarity to God. For example, God is the Holy One, who cannot commit sin. Human beings are also holy, who hate to commit sins. Human beings are precious because they are like God. The more we emphasize human dignity, the more human beings can develop their potential. We can find bad examples all over the world where people are disregarded and treated as mere objects. These sins include human trafficking, unfair labor practices, elitism, and abusive economic policies, just to name a few. People are despised and they are robbed of their dignity and the chance to develop their potential. Under harsh governments' control, people lose their chance to use and develop their potential, because they have to work so hard to make a living.

One of the main themes of the Bible is the dignity of human beings. From the beginning, God created human beings and loved them. The three persons in Matthew 1:1 (Jesus Christ, David, and Abraham) deeply recognized human dignity. They acknowledged human dignity regardless of their social position and station. Regardless of a high or low social position, good or bad, male or female, rich or poor, they respected human dignity. They regarded human beings as precious because they were human. When people were sick, poor, weak or wicked, the three persons in Matthew 1:1 still believed human beings were precious. How can it be possible for the three persons of Matthew 1:1 to believe this way? The reason is very simple. Abraham, David, and Jesus Christ understood God's thoughts in an insightful ways. When they saw people, they saw people through God's eyes, not in their own sight. It is one reason why their names were written in the beginning of the New Testament.

Precious Abraham

Where can we find the example of when Abraham sees human dignity like God does? We can find one example in his relationship with his nephew Lot. Abraham and Lot could not stay together because of the increase of their livestock. So, Lot chose for himself the whole plain of the Jordan and set out toward the East. The two men parted company (Gen 13:10-11). Lot did not give much thought about Abraham's feelings and needs. He just chose Sodom, which was well watered, like the garden of the LORD, like the land of Egypt. Lot's behavior seemed selfish.

In a short time, Lot got into trouble. There was an outbreak of war in Lot's land. It was a big war. At this time Amraphel king of Shinar, Arioch king of Ellasar, Kedorlaomer king of Elam, and Tidal king of Goiim went to war against Bera king of Sodom, Birsha king of Gomorrah, Shinab king of Admah, Shemeber king of Zeboiim, and the king of Bela (that is, Zoar) (Gen 14:1-2). Unfortunately, the five kings' armies on Lot's side, were defeated by the enemies. The four kings seized all the goods of Sodom and Gomorrah and all their food; then they went away. They also carried off Abram's nephew Lot and his possessions, since he was living in Sodom (Gen 14:11-12).

If Abraham saw Lot from a selfish point of view, he would not have helped Lot. Although Abraham knew that Lot was selfish and cunning, Abraham remembered that Lot also was a precious human being, who was created in God's image. Abraham could not leave him in his miserable conditions. When Abraham heard that his relative had been taken captive, he called out the 318 trained men born into his household and went in pursuit of them as far as Dan. He recovered all the goods and brought back his relative Lot and his possessions, together with the women and the other people (Gen 14:14-16).

If Abraham had not helped to rescue Lot and his family, what would have happened to them? They definitely would have been sold as slaves. If they had become slaves, they would have been treated like property with no human dignity. Their lives would be full of hunger, physical suffering, loneliness, and bitter tears. When they died, their bodies would have been cast away like animals.

However, Abraham did not abandon Lot and his families' lives because of their dignity. Abraham recognized that Lot was a precious human being, who was created in God's image. Abraham overcame any negative feelings toward Lot and decided to help him. In other words, Abraham succeeded to see Lot from God's viewpoint. Abraham ran a great risk to rescue Lot and his family. What was his risk?

Abraham risked his own life and the lives of the other 318 people under his command. Although he won the battle, it was a risky battle by going against four kings' armies. How can we compare Abraham's 318 people to four kings' armies? However, Abraham and his 318 people planned a surprise attack on their enemies at night. God helped Abraham because Abraham tried to help God's precious creation, Lot, who was downtrodden.

Precious David

Where can we find the example of when King David's sees human dignity like God does? We can find the example in the relationship between David and Saul. At the time, Saul was king of Israel and David was his subject. However, when God helped David and David won the Israelite people's favor, a problem arose (1 Sam 18:16). Saul was jealous of David's popularity with the people. Since Saul envied David so much, he decided to kill David. First, Saul tried to impale David by hurling his spear at him, while muttering to himself, "I'll pin David to the wall." Next Saul gathered his army and tried to kill David, but David eluded him twice more (1 Sam 18:11, 19:10). Fortunately, David was not killed by Saul, but he had to hide from him. He became a fugitive, who had to wander and hide. If he did not have his good friend, Jonathan, he would have been killed by Saul. Jonathan, King Saul's son, loved David and helped him many times to escape "the valley of death" (1 Sam 20:42).

There were at least three reasons, why Saul should not have tried to kill David. The first reason is that David was truly a loyal subject who helped and served Saul. Whenever a spirit of depression came upon Saul, David would take his harp and play. Then relief would come to Saul, he would feel better, and the evil spirit would leave him (1 Sam 16:23).

The second reason was that David gave Saul big victories in the battle with the Philistines. In the battle with the Philistines, Saul's army was scattered and almost defeated by the Philistines army. In that time, little David, who came to the battle field to serve his brothers, fought with Goliath, the invincible giant warrior of the Philistines. As David depended on God for the victory, he killed Goliath and gave a miraculous victory to Saul. Saul was indebted to David because of the great victory. (1 Sam 17:53-54)

The third reason was the personal relationship between Saul and David. Saul appointed David as a commander of a thousand men. Saul also made David his son-in-law (1 Sam 18:27). However, Saul's intentions were not pure. He also tried to kill David through this personal relationship. Saul asked David to kill a hundred Philistines as his marriage gift to wed his daughter. Saul hoped that David would be killed by the Philistines when he went to complete the task.

On the other hand, David had two chances to kill Saul. He did not kill him, but instead David just cut off a corner of Saul's robe (1 Sam 24:4). In the second chance, he just took Saul's spear and water jug (1 Sam 26:12). Why did David not kill Saul, who did not appreciate David's loyalty? It was because of human dignity. Human dignity comes from God. God created, chose, and anointed Saul as the king of Israel, so David did not kill Saul.

Precious Jesus Christ

There were so many examples during Jesus Christ's earthly life that showed He considered human beings as God's precious creatures. We can find three examples in the book of John. The first one is the meeting with Nicodemus (Jn 3:1-15). Although Nicodemus was a high religious leader in Israel, he could not solve his conversion problem. He sought the way of his soul's salvation, although he had not found the answer, he earnestly sought it. That is the reason why he visited Jesus in the middle of the night. Nicodemus was a religious person in his outer appearance, but he was still an unconverted sinner on the inside. When he visited Jesus Christ, he heard the Gospel from Jesus: "Just as Moses lifted up the snake in the desert, so the Son of Man must be lifted up that everyone who believes in him may have eternal life" (Jn 3:14-15). Although Nicodemus was a sinner, Jesus considered him as precious and gave him God's wonderful message of salvation.

The second person is the Samaritan woman, who Jesus met at Jacob's well (Jn 4:3-26). She was a deeply, morally corrupted woman. She had five husbands, but the man she was living with at that time was not her husband. She was left out in the cold by Jewish people and even Samarian people, because she was so morally corrupted. She could not solve her problems of loneliness, identity, and low self-esteem. Jesus Christ considered her as a very precious person. Although she faced troubles in her life, Jesus knew that she was also created in God's image.

Why did Jesus visit this town? I believe that Jesus visited this town to meet her and recover her dignity as God's precious person. Jesus made a long journey of about 50 miles, to meet her in the desert. Finally, he met her, changed her, and recovered her human dignity.

The third case was the meeting with the man, who had suffered for 38 years (Jn 5:2). This person had suffered from a disease for 38 years. His body had been broken deeply for a long time. He had only one desire, which was the restoration of his health. However, he failed to find the way of healing. His friends and his family gave up hope for his healing. Even his homeless friends had abandoned him. He had no hope. He existed in utter despair. However, Jesus Christ did not abandon him! He saw God's image in the dirty, hopeless patient. He found human dignity in the person, who was lost in despair. Jesus met him at the pool of Bethesda, which was full of various patients. Then, Jesus healed his disease and forgave his sins. Jesus restored his human dignity, and the man could go back to his family.

"Precious Me" in the Image of God

Throughout the Bible we learned that Abraham, David, and Jesus respected the human dignity of God's creation. The basis of their human dignity is simply that God created them in His image. We can learn three lessons from Abraham, David, and Jesus' respect of human dignity.

The first lesson is that we should risk our lives to save God's people as Abraham risked his life to save his nephew Lot. Abraham did not risk his life for other people, but for Lot, who was considered by God to be Abraham's responsibility. Just like Abraham, we cannot risk our lives for all people. However, we should risk our lives for the people for whom we have responsibility. As Abraham saved Lot from the enemies, we should save God's people from the temptations of the world. Some people are morally corrupted or broken off from the Christian community. Many turn against God and try to live by his or her own strength and will. Others are driven by evil spirits. Some ridicule the Christian faith and are engrossed into other religions. No matter what their situations are, they were also created in God's image and they are God's precious people. When we meet them, we should recognize their dignity and should risk our lives to save them. What does it mean to risk our lives for them? It means that we may not be loved and respected by them, and maybe even persecuted by them. However, if we really deny ourselves and respect their human dignity, God could save them from their darkness.

The second lesson is that just like David did not take revenge on Saul, we must respect the people who hurt us and attack us. The people who hurt and attack us are also God's precious creation who has been made in God's image. Although they afflict us following the worldly customs and evil spirits, we should not hate them. Rather, we should forgive them and bless them. There are too many people who do not understand human dignity in the world. Because people do not understand this truth, people hurt, lie about, and afflict each other. Christians also live together with these people. So, Christians are also hurt by the people who try to take advantage of Christians. Christians are also tempted to hate and get revenge against them. However, Christians should not forget the deep meaning of human dignity. Only God can take revenge. The Apostle Paul reminds us: "Do not take revenge, my friends, but leave room for God's wrath, for it is written: 'It is mine to avenge; I will repay,' says the Lord" (Rom 12:19). Like this, Christians should allow God to take revenge on the wicked and further should try to help them because they are God's precious creatures. The Apostle Paul commanded us: "If your enemy is hungry, feed him; if he is thirsty, give him something to drink. In doing this, you will heap burning coals on his head" (Rom 12:20). What are the burning coals? These are the burning coals of conviction of sin, to turn away from evil, turn to God, and do what is right.

God intervened in the relationship between Saul and David. God punished Saul, who committed sins continually through the Philistines. The Philistines killed Saul cruelly (1 Sam 31:5). What was David's response to the cruel death of Saul? Was he happy with the news of Saul's death? No. David felt sorry and fasted when he heard of the death of Saul. The reason is simple. For David, Saul was not only the king of Israel, but also God's precious person, who was also made in the image of God.

The third lesson is that Jesus Christ respected all people as God's precious creation, no matter how corrupt morally, spiritually, or bodily. As Jesus did, we should respect our neighbors as God's precious people. How can we respect their dignity? The answer is what Jesus did for them. We should act like Jesus Christ. Jesus restored their dignity through meeting them. There are too many people, who are corrupted spiritually, morally, and bodily. Although they are created in God's image, they do not know their dignity and their identity. The reason for this situation is very simple. They live their lives apart from God, and do not know their value. We do not have any power or method which makes people come back to God. In many cases, they do not know they have wandered away toward the corrupted world. We should recover their dignity, which is part of God's glory. The way of restoration for their dignity is introducing Jesus to them. Jesus Christ restored the dignity of Nicodemus, the Samaritan woman, and the patient of 38 years' through the power of the gospel. We can restore our neighbors' dignity and preciousness by introducing them to Jesus Christ, who is our Savior and Healer.

Chapter 8

The Life of a Nomad

"An account of the genealogy of Jesus the Messiah, the son of David, the son of Abraham" (Matthew 1:1, NRSV).

Life may be compared to the life of a wanderer. What could be the reason? We can understand the reason easily if we recognize the meaning of the term "nomad." A nomad is a person who has left one's hometown and wanders about from place to place. Everyone who is born in this world travels from place to place.

As I look back on my life, I realize that it is true. I have migrated to several places during my life. I was born and raised in Seoul, Korea, and have lived at Jang-Dan City in Kyoung-Gi province, and Ye-San City in Chung-Nam province to get away from the Korean War. I lived in Kang-Won and Jun-Ra province during my time in the military. After I became a Christian, I continued to live my life as a wanderer. I have always roamed from place to place such as Thailand, USA, India, Korea, and so on.

The three people that are mentioned in the verse, Abraham, David, and Jesus, were no exception to this nomadic lifestyle. They were people who moved from place to place. Even though they had a physical hometown, their hometown was not overly significant for them after they became an adult. This is because they were not people who were stuck in past. They considered the present to be as important as the past.

Abraham, David, and Jesus Christ thought the present was important, although they could not live a comfortable life in the present. They knew that the present was not everything, but also that there is an abundant life in the future. It is very significant that the future is dualistic. This is because there are two kinds of the future: the future in the present and the future after one's death. Moreover, the future is more important because it is an eternal one.

Abraham the Nomad

Before Abraham met God, he moved from Ur of the Chaldeans to Haran (Gen 11:31). After the death of his father in Haran, he moved to Shechem, present-day Israel, as he obeyed the word of the Lord (Gen 12:5). His journey was about 621 miles long. He went down to Egypt to live there (Gen 12:10). Then he then came back from Egypt to Hebron. So did he live in peace at Hebron? Of course not!

Abraham has constantly wandered without a permanent settlement. He went to the north side, and then came back to Hebron again. He went to Beersheba through Gerar, but came back to Hebron again since his circumstances changed. Abraham's nomadic life can be placed into three periods. The first is from the Chaldeans to Israel, the second is going to and coming back from Egypt and third is wandering in Israel. Through his itinerant life, he bought a track of land and a burial ground. However, he did not just live within the boundaries of his property on this earth.

If that was the case, what sustained Abraham during his life as a wanderer? Quite simply, it was hope. To which hope did he hold on? That was the hope of his hometown. Does this mean that Abraham had hope in Ur of the Chaldeans where he was born? Of course not! The earthly and physical hometown could be a place of reminiscence, but it could not be the place of hope. If that is so, in which town did Abraham hope?

The writer of Hebrews described Abraham's hometown: "All these people were still living by faith when they died. They did not receive the things promised; they only saw them and welcomed them from a distance. And they admitted that they were aliens and strangers on earth....If they have been thinking of the country they had left, they would have had opportunity to return. Instead, they were longing for a better country - a heavenly one. Therefore God is not ashamed to be called their God, for he has prepared a city for them" (Heb 11:13-16).

Who are *all these people* in the passage? They are Abraham, his wife, Sarah, his son and grandson. The Bible continues, "By faith he made his home in the promised land like a stranger in a foreign country; he lived in tents, as did Isaac and Jacob, who were heirs with him of the same promise. For he was looking forward to the city with foundations, whose architect and builder is God" (Heb 11: 9-10).

Even though life on earth was the life of a nomad to Abraham, he knew that he would ultimately return to his true hometown, which was the heavenly country that God prepared. The heavenly country is a perfect and eternal place. Due to this hope, he did not mind living the life of a wanderer. Living with the faithful family who had the same hope was a great comfort to him. To long for this fellowship with his family was very valuable for him; it was fellowship in the heavenly country. Abraham and his family could tolerate their "wandering" lifestyle laughing and crying together because of the same hope.

David the Nomad

David had lived a nomadic life like Abraham did. His life as a wanderer can be divided into four periods. In the first period, the center of David's life was Gibeah. He had helped Saul come and go between Bethlehem and Gibeah. David fought several wars and finally became aware of Saul's plot to kill him, but David escaped Saul by leaving Gibeah (1 Sam Ch 16-22).

David's second period of a wandering lifestyle was the time of fleeing from Saul. During this period, he had been filled with foreboding and roved over the mountains, the wilderness, and hid in caves. Despite his wretched circumstances, David rescued his parents from danger (1 Sam 22:3-4), met a beautiful woman, Abigail, destroyed the Amalekites and recovered everything the Amalekites had stolen (1 Sam Ch 22-30).

The third period of David's peripatetic lifestyle was after Saul died. David returned from his refuge in Ziklag to Hebron. After David became King over Israel, he conquered Jerusalem, which became his headquarters. David traveled from Jerusalem several times. He went to Baal Perazim, and there he defeated the Philistines who worshiped idols. He went to Baalah of Judah to bring up from there the Ark of God (2 Sam Ch 5-6).

David's fourth period of the lifestyle of a nomad was after he brought the kingdom under a single authority. Thereafter he unified the northern kingdom of Israel and the southern kingdom of Judah, and could live at peace in Jerusalem, the capital. However, he chose the life of a wanderer. Why did he do that? Because he wanted to expand his territory. David set out on his journey in order to defeat the Moabites, to occupy Zobah, to annihilate the Amalekites, and to do battle with the Ammonites. He also fled Jerusalem to escape from Absalom (2 Sam Ch 8-19).

What sustained David's lifestyle of a rambler? For David, like Abraham, it was hope. What hope did he have? It was through the promise that God appointed David as the king of Israel. As God's voucher, God anointed him through Samuel (1 Sam 16:13). David willingly put up with the life of a wanderer facing all kinds of troubles because he had hope that he would be the king and rule over the people who God would entrust to him.

David had many supporters who had the same hope, both in joy and in sorrow. He had been with people who fled, starved, ate, slept on a field, cried, and laughed together. Their number was about four hundred (1 Sam 22:1-2). Leading these people could have been a heavy burden to David when his enemies pursued him. He did not treat them as a burden, but rather stopped his dangerous drifting ways to comfort and help them.

Jesus Christ the Nomad

How was the life of Jesus Christ? He, as the Son of God, was blessed with the glory of heaven. He, the Most High, came into our world in a lowly state. He lived as a homeless wanderer. His hometown was the kingdom of heaven, where there was no sin, disease, or poverty. There was no jealousy, anger, hatred, and murder in that place. Instead, it was a place full of peace, holiness, and glory.

Jesus, who came to this earth, lived life as a literal wanderer. He had "no place to lay his head." In one sense, His life was worse than the birds of the air and the foxes of the mountains (Mt 8-20). Jesus who created this world and everything in the world sometimes did not have food to eat (Mt 12:1). He continually had to wander from here to there like Abraham and David did.

Jesus' nomadic life can be split into three stages. The first stage was when Jesus was taken by his parents to Egypt (Mt 2:14) because King Herod wanted to kill him. This refugee life began shortly after he was born, and was to be a foreshadowing of his difficult life. Jesus' second stage of a wandering life was when he returned to Jerusalem after King Herod died. Jesus had to withdraw to Nazareth in order to flee from the son of Herod, who took over his father's throne.

The third stage was when Jesus began his ministry. He went throughout the land to meet people who needed him. He went from place to place to meet people no matter who they were or what they had. He went to Capernaum from Jerusalem and back to Jerusalem from Capernaum. Jesus even went to Samaria where others were reluctant to go, to Mt. Hermon, and the Decapolis, where it was surrounded by hills, valleys, and other hostile elements.

For Jesus, what hope led him to his wandering life? He had the same hope as Abraham and David had. Jesus' hope was the salvation of humankind. His hope was to save people who lived without hope. Jesus did not refuse his wandering life because his life would point the people who lived without direction and knowledge to the place where their wandering life would eventually come to an end.

Jesus Christ had a spiritual intimate relationship with the God of hope. He received spiritual power from God the Father to make his hope strong. He was also able to live nomadically, because he had a relationship with his disciples who shared and inherited his hope. If Jesus had had no disciples, then who would have carried on Jesus' message and lifestyle of hope? The most tragic thing would have been to see God's hope fade.

"Me" the Nomad

The Gospel of Mathew Chapter one is a genealogy of three persons; that is Abraham, David, and Jesus Christ. The similarity of these three persons is that they accepted their nomadic lives. They did not mind the life of a wanderer, but endured their life because of a hope that was given to them. Their lives are an inspiration to all Christians. Throughout their lives as wanderers, we may find at least three lessons to apply to our lives.

The first lesson is that we have to live with hope for the kingdom of God as Abraham, David and Jesus did. This world in which we are living is not our eternal hometown. Someday we all are supposed to depart from this world. Those who have hope in the kingdom of heaven will enter their eternal hometown on the day we depart this world. However, those who do not have hope for the kingdom will not be able to enter the city of God.

People who choose the kingdom of heaven as their home are usually misunderstood and receive criticism from people who settle in this world as their home. This is a natural consequence because our thought, speech and behavior are different from theirs. We do not give priority to this world and the ways of this world. Therefore, it is a natural result that we are mocked by those who give priority to this world and to the ways of this world. Peter describes it, "For you have spent enough time in the past doing what pagans choose to do--living in debauchery, lust, drunkenness, orgies, carousing and detestable idolatry. They think it strange that you do not plunge with them into the same flood of dissipation, and they heap abuse on you. But they will have to give account to him who is ready to judge the living and the dead" (1 Pet 4:3-5). What an accurate but a terrifying portrayal of reality.

While Abraham lived the pilgrim life, there were families of faith that went with Abraham and consoled him. Similarly, Christians should live in fellowship with families of faith that have hope for the kingdom of heaven. In the house in which we share our faith, we have to share not only the same hope but also the tears and joys. We should share our time and our material, as well as our hearts. Through fellowship, we can receive a taste of the eternal fellowship which we will enjoy in heaven.

The second lesson is that we have to live holding onto the promises that God gave us. David lived the wanderer's life with hope in the promises of God. Even though David muddled through the bitter journeys of life, he overcame his present suffering because of the strength he gained from all his previous sufferings. Likewise, we have the promise of God. The promise is that "As you come to him, the living Stone, you also, like living stones, are being built into a spiritual house" (1 Pet 2:4-5).

People who belong to San Dol Church take hold to the wanderer's life because of the words of His promise. We could comfortably live a pious life attending a church located nearby our homes. We also could attend a church that takes pride in good facilities and systems. However, we chose a wanderer's life instead of a comfortable life and faith. Even though San Dol Church simply began to worship at a layperson's house, there was a loving fellowship in the church.

When we had a worship service at a classroom in Ewha Middle School, attached to Ewha Women's University, the church was in a poor environment. In spite of the fact that this small auditorium was much better than the classroom, we are still worshipping under poor circumstances. Why did we choose this wanderer's life? This is because we have hope that the promise of God is going to be accomplished. Like David, who shared hope with 400 refugees, we as the church family are like refugees, wanderers who live crying, laughing, pushing, and pulling for together.

If we become San Dol, which is translated in English to mean "living-stone," are built as a church faithful to our duties in our own position, and grounded like a living stone, praying and caring for each other from the bottom of our hearts like living stones, God will bring many people together into our church. Of course an important matter is not the number but the nature of wanderer's life. I would hope that you form yourselves as the promise of God in this church.

The third lesson is that we should not mind a wanderer's life as we hope for the salvation of our neighbors. Jesus Christ chose a wanderer's life because of a hope for salvation of all humankind. Jesus Christ lived a life of sacrifice and poverty for the salvation of all humankind. We should also live a lifestyle of sacrifice for the salvation of our neighbors. We have to pray for them and should visit them. We must form good connections with them, and share sacrificially to meet their needs just like Jesus did.

In order to share hope, Jesus Christ prayed continually and shared spiritual fellowship with God the Father. Likewise, having ultimate hope for the salvation of our neighborhoods, we should pray and share spiritual fellowship with God the Father. Our souls would dry up without prayer. We will lose peace and joy, as well as our love and compassion. Instead, we will be filled with unbelief and conflict without fellowship with God the Father.

Jesus Christ did not keep his hope to himself. He distributed hope to his disciples because it was so precious. After he took the twelve disciples, he gave the mission of salvation of all humankind to them. Likewise, God gave us hope, salvation for sinners. We cannot store up and keep the hope for ourselves. We should share this precious hope to our neighborhoods.

How can we share this hope effectively? The answer is that we just do as Jesus did. He chose a small number of people, and shared hope while enjoying good fellowship with them. Likewise, we have to choose a few persons among our neighborhoods and share our lives with them. We should enjoy good fellowship with them, plant hope in them and make them to be His disciples. It is worth that we live this life, even though we live life as nomads.

Chapter 9

Be Prepared

"An account of the genealogy of Jesus the Messiah, the son of David, the son of Abraham." (Matthew. 1:1, NRSV).

Although we live a life as a pilgrimage, we can make it worthwhile. How can we transform it to be worthy and meaningful? There are many ways. One of them, like the Boy Scout motto, is to "be prepared." How can we transform our life of pilgrimage into a worthy one through preparation? The answer is simple. The opportunity comes to the one who is prepared.

While we are living this life, an opportunity comes to us. The opportunity would be available to everyone of all ages and genders. It could be good or bad. The prepared one could catch it and rise to a higher level of life. On the contrary, the one who is not prepared could not use it, or at best just stumble over it.

The very first three persons of the Book of Matthew, Abraham, David, and Jesus Christ, also had an opportunity. They encountered crises at times and opportunity at other times. Abraham, David and Jesus Christ caught and used it whether it was a problem or a possibility. As a consequence, they were able to go higher developmentally, socially, and spiritually.

How did Abraham, David, and Jesus Christ take and apply opportunities? They have no special means. They were being prepared themselves in their daily lives. Of course, they did not know every kind of crisis that they would face to prepare specifically for it. They lived and prepared themselves according to the principles of the Bible. Therefore, our daily preparation is something so important which can change our life entirely.

Abraham Prepared

What kind of crisis did Abraham encounter? It was when Abraham heard the allied forces from four countries captured his nephew Lot. Let's hear the Word of God directly, "They also carried off Abram's nephew Lot and his possessions, since he was living in Sodom" (Gen 14:12, NIV). When Abraham heard of this news, what could he do? He was a 75-year old man. He was neither a soldier nor a politician. If he was a soldier, he could use military power. If he was a politician, he could do his best for Lot's life through all the wiles of diplomacy.

If Abraham had been a rich man, he would have used his money as a ransom for Lot. But Abraham was only a nomad who cared for sheep and cattle. He had little money. Then, how did Abraham get back Lot and Lot's family? The secret was his preparation. He was an ordinary nomad, but in terms of his thorough preparation, he was not an ordinary nomad. He was a man living according to the principles of the Bible. Then what and how did Abraham prepare? Look at the Scripture again, in order to find how he had prepared.

> When Abram heard that his relative had been taken captive, he called out the 318 trained men born in his household and went in pursuit as far as Dan. During the night Abram divided his men to attack them and he routed them, pursuing them as far as Hobah, north of Damascus. He recovered all the goods and brought back his relative Lot and his possessions, together with the women and the other people." (Gen 14:14-16, NIV)

How did Abraham prepare himself during his daily life? He prepared the people daily. In these verses, we find a phrase "trained men born in his household." What does this phrase mean? Obviously, Abraham trained his people in ordinary times. Then, how did he prepare them? According to this phrase, two methods can be found. First, a clue was found from "born in his household." Abraham must have had many people in his household. Abraham must have maintained his household in such a way that they grew up in good health. Abraham, who honored God, must have created a proper environment for physical and spiritual health for his people. If they had not been healthy, how could they have defeated the four kings and all the allied forces?

The second clue was found in the word "trained." Abraham not only provided a good environment for his people, but also trained them. Abraham did not waste his precious time but trained his people daily. Abraham must have trained them not only physically, but also mentally and spiritually. Without physical and mental training, they could not have attacked the four kings and allied forces.

David Prepared

Now let's look at David. David's life was full of ups and downs. He encountered many crises, even near death circumstances. On the other hand, David had opportunities, too. Whenever the opportunities came, he did not miss them and finally became a king of united Israel.

So how did David properly deal with the crises and opportunities? How did he prepare? Like Abraham before him, David trained his people. The training of the people was a part of David's own preparation. There were named thirty-seven heroes of David in 2 Samuel 23:8. They were trained by David in ordinary times, but showed their bravery at every step with David. David's people had the same bravery and piety of David. They went into battle and won with him. Finally, they were praiseworthy allies, who made David king of a united Israel and supported the kingdom and reign of David. Then they dedicated themselves to the expansion of David's kingdom.

However, David's people had various contributions to make. Some killed many enemies, some found what David needed to forget about his life, some rescued David from wild beasts, and some were not mentioned for what they did. Even though every soldier's duty and capacity was different, their allegiance and devotion to David was equal. They were named in the Bible, and David also remembered them.

An interesting part of the background of David's supporters was that they were from every area of Israel and even included Arbites, Ammonites, and Hittites. In other words, there were people in this group who traditionally hated the Israelites. David measured their devotion and commitment rather than their ethnic background. David shared his glory with his people who had David's faith and training.

There were two reasons why David achieved fame in spite of his life full of ups and downs. One was his faith regarding the promise of God and his belief that God would make it happen. Another reason was the complete devotion of his people. With these two elements David won the victory against his enemies and gained renown, which he shared with his leaders by including each of his names in his records.

Jesus Christ Prepared

How was Jesus Christ prepared? The life of Jesus was too short. He did not live as long as Abraham, nor did he have any offspring. He would not have a political kingdom in this world like David had. He was miserably killed on the cross when he was just over thirty. His body was torn and His blood was shed on the cross. It was such a cruel death.

Because of His early death, Jesus Christ's preparation was urgent and needed to be perfect. If not, his important calling for world evangelization would perish with His death. For this reason, Jesus started to train His people as soon as he began His public ministry. First, He chose His disciples (Mt 4:18-22). Then He trained his disciples. The training of Jesus Christ was to share His life and calling.

We already know the purpose of the incarnation of Jesus Christ. It was world evangelization. But Jesus had no international experience. He had only one experience when he fled to Egypt in His parents' arms to escape being murdered by King Herod. So, how could He evangelize the entire world? The only way was through His disciples. For this reason, Jesus trained His disciples with all His might.

You might be surprised to know the background of the twelve disciples that Jesus chose and trained. Except for one, they were rural people from Galilee. Judas, the one from the upper class, committed suicide because of his guilt in betraying Jesus. Although they had no academic background or high social status, the other eleven disciples of Jesus received training from Jesus Christ.

After their training, the disciples of Jesus proclaimed the gospel of Jesus with all their heart, soul, mind and strength. They did not despise any the loss or seek any worldly gain. They were not deterred by their environment. They offered their life to Jesus Christ who trained and shared the calling for world evangelization with them. They placed a higher value on their calling for evangelization than their life. Finally, they gave up their life to gain the whole world.

What is the result? Above all, Jesus Christ was glorified. Because of the disciples who he chose and trained, Jesus Christ is glorified all over the world. Many people confess Jesus Christ as their Lord and Savior. Incidentally, the disciples of Jesus also are honored, because wherever the name of Christ has gone, the names of disciples also are known there.

Am I Prepared?

In today's Scripture, we learned the following lessons: First, in ordinary times, Abraham trained his 318 people. Because Abraham was ready in ordinary times, he could deal with the crisis of the kidnapped of his nephew and family. He changed the crisis into an opportunity. It became a turning point of his life. From that time forward, Abraham entered into deeper conversation and relationship with God (Gen 15:1).

We are similarly called. We have to train our children. Indeed, all parents are trying to teach their children the right way. But, we Christians must train our offspring in the principles of God. Therefore, we have to provide a good and healthy environment for them. Above all, parent's lifestyle is crucial, because the kids will learn from their parent's life.

Second, David also trained his people in his ordinary times. He trained them in piety first, and then trained them for combat. David and the people shared the sweet and bitter times of life together, and the soldiers devoted themselves to him until the end. As a result, God was glorified, because the promise of God was fulfilled. David was honored, because he became a king of united Israel. Finally, the people of David were honored, because each of them got an important position in David's kingdom.

Likewise for us, just as David trained his people in ordinary times and taught them to be brave, we also have to be trained and train others. We must live as we are trained and strive for the expansion of God's kingdom. We should never make light of our training. If a trainee did not practice what he/she had learned, it would come to nothing.

Third, Jesus Christ had trained twelve disciples during His ministry. His teaching style was unique. He became a role model of the disciples. He not only shared his mission unconditionally, but He gave his life for them. To make a long story short, Jesus' life is the way to train disciples.

The same thing goes for us. We have to be trained in a small group. After the training, we have to train our own groups. This is a quicker way to expand the kingdom of heaven. Small group training is the most solid way of training. If a Christian did not train in a small group, he/she could not be a good leader. In addition, a person may more easily resist committing sin, if he/she follows Jesus Christ's example.

Abraham, David, and Jesus Christ have trained their people in ordinary times. However, Jesus Christ trained only twelve in contrast to Abraham's 318 and David's 37. Why is this? Did Abraham and David have more ability than Jesus Christ? No. Abraham's training was only for winning a battle. David did not train his people only for a battle, but for governing a nation after the battle, and after the responsibilities had been conceded to them.

In contrast, Jesus Christ's training is not just a physical training, but it is spiritual as well. Consequently, the disciples of Jesus became outstanding spiritual leaders. In this example, the size of a small group is important, because a small group allows more solid training of its members. If a person wants to be a spiritual leader, he/she should be trained in a small group. To be trained as a spiritual leader is more crucial than Abraham's or David's training.

Once we examine the training of Abraham, David, and Jesus Christ, we note that the intensity was quite different. Abraham's training was rather easy. For this reason the trainees were used only one time. David's training was harder than Abraham's. It was a life threatening training. So they were used repeatedly and they got their rewards. Jesus Christ's training was the most solid and the toughest. When the disciples started their training, they had to give up all their possessions, they left their families, and they abandoned their right for fame or wealth in the world. But there is no one who has affected human history like the disciples of Jesus. Through them, many people have been saved and found the purpose of life. Churches are planted all over the world. Above all, many people are living holy and sacrificial lives to help others.

So, which training should be ours? Would you be included in the 318 or the 37 people, or would you rather be trained like the disciples of Jesus? Now, the choice is in our hands. No one will choose it for us and no one can be trained for us. If we make the right choice and "be prepared," God will bless you for it and bring the kingdom through your hands.

Chapter 10

The Genealogy of Life or Death

"An account of the genealogy of Jesus the Messiah, the son of David, the son of Abraham" (Matthew 1:1, NRSV).

The second word in Matthew 1:1, *genealogy*, is rather interesting, because the original Greek word can be translated in a few different ways. If the word is used only to introduce the following paragraph, genealogy is rightly put. The reason is simple! The paragraph from verse 2 to verse 17 is the list of Jesus Christ's ancestors. It is also possible to translate the word as origin, meaning the story of Jesus' birth. The word can be translated as history or creation, depending upon how it is used.

Davies and Allison, in their commentary, suggest the possibility of rendering the word in different ways as follows:

> [Matthew] 1:1 is telescopic: it can be extended to include more and more of what Matthew is beginning to write about. First, it can cover the genealogy which immediately follows it; then, it can refer to the account of the birth of Jesus…; third, it can mean 'history' or 'life story'; finally, it can refer to the whole new creation which begins at the conception of Jesus and will be completed at his second coming.[1]

Two Genealogies

There are only two places where the Bible displays a genealogy, specifically mentioning 'the book of the genealogy' in the Bible. Although there are many genealogies in the Bible, there are no

---

[1] W. D. Davies & Dale C. Allison, *A Critical & Exegetical Commentary on the Gospel according to Saint Matthew*, vol. 1 (Edinburgh: T. & T. Clark Limited, 1988), 154.

genealogies that use the term "the book" like these two genealogies. One is Matthew 1:1, and the other is Genesis 5:1. "This is the book of the genealogy of Adam."

If we look into these two genealogies thoroughly we can find several interesting facts. First, Genesis 5:1 mentions the genealogy of Adam, and Matthew 1:1 mentions the genealogy of Jesus Christ. The genealogy is significant because Adam was the first man. God created Adam and made him the forefather of all mankind. When God created Adam in His image, He called him "man" (Gen 5:2).

The way in which God created Adam is noteworthy. The Bible says, "The LORD God formed the man from the dust of the ground and breathed into his nostrils the breath of life, and the man became a living being" (Gen 2:7 KJV). According to this verse, God created Adam with His own hands and personally breathed the breath of life into him. Here 'the breath of life' means the Holy Spirit. Since then, God has not created any person in the same way that He made Adam. God never breathed the breath of life "personally" into anyone else as He did for Adam.

Similarly, the birth of Jesus Christ was different from that of any other person. Jesus Christ was the only person for whom God directly participated in the birth. How did God participate? First of all, God appeared to Mary and announced that she would have a baby. Afterwards, Mary conceived and gave birth to Jesus by the Holy Spirit as God had promised.

There is a point of similarity between the birth of Adam and that of Jesus: God's direct involvement through the Holy Spirit. These two births were different from that of all other people. Every human being has been born by the union between a husband and a wife. However, the first man Adam and Jesus Christ were both born by the direct engagement of God through the Holy Spirit. All in all, these two genealogies are the records of two special people who were born by God's deliberate activity.

Contrasting Genealogies

1. The Genealogy of Adam

The second reason these two genealogies are interesting may be seen in contrasting their different emphases. In order to find the emphases, consider Genesis 5:3-4: "And Adam lived an hundred and thirty years, and begat a son in his own likeness, and after his image; and called his name Seth: And the days of Adam after he had begotten Seth were eight hundred years: and he begat sons and daughters:" (KJV).

According to these verses, Adam had begotten many children. To emphasize this fact, the Bible repeatedly uses the verb "beget" three times. The expression "beget a child" means produce a new life. It means that a precious person created in the image of God was born. A man has immeasurable potential because he has been created in the image of God. As a man grows, that man can be a truly great person.

Therefore, the birth of a human being is a great blessing. Everyone rejoices in it together. People remember and celebrate together someone's birthday until he or she dies. However, the man cannot celebrate forever. Someday he has to leave this world. Even Adam did not live forever. The Bible says, "And all the days that Adam lived were nine hundred and thirty years: and he died" (Gen 5:5, KJV).

In short, the genealogy of Adam is the record of death. Every person in this genealogy was born into this world. They also tasted the joy of receiving children. However, whether they were healthy or not, happy or not—they died. Some lived long, others did not. Adam died and his sons died, too. The tenth descendent Noah also died.

The genealogy of Adam in Genesis 5 is the genealogy of death. Of course, the seventh descendent of Adam, Enoch, walked with God and did not see death. But everyone else in this genealogy consistently experienced death. The verb "beget" appears 27 times in the genealogy. What does it mean? Although it seems a man in this genealogy loved, married, and lived happily, this genealogy shows us the frightening truth that no one can avoid death.

2. The Genealogy of Jesus Christ

Now, let's go back to Matthew, chapter 1. As I said before, this is the genealogy of Jesus Christ. People in this genealogy beget children, just as Adam's descendants did. The verb "beget" also appears 40 times, and like the genealogy of Adam, a man in this genealogy loved, married, and lived happily. However, there is a big difference between Jesus' genealogy and the genealogy of Adam: there is no mention of "death."

Does the fact that death is not mentioned mean that the 42 people listed in the genealogy of Jesus Christ did not die? Of course, they grew old and died. But if so, why does this genealogy not include that they died? The reason is this: Even though they died from a human perspective, God does not consider them dead, because there is no expression of death.

Let me explain this very important truth. Every human being born into this world eventually dies. However, life does not end with physical death. According to the Bible, there is a life of resurrection after death. There are two kinds of life in resurrection. One is the resurrection of judgment. The other is the resurrection of life. In other words, some people receive judgment after resurrection. Others, however, receive eternal life without judgment.

If there are two resurrections, what is the standard to distinguish between the resurrection of life and that of judgment? The genealogy to which a person belongs determines it. As we have already examined, people in the genealogy of Adam not only die, but are also put into hell after judgment. However, people in the genealogy of Jesus Christ enter into eternal life after death. For this reason, the genealogy of Jesus Christ did not express that people *died* because they belonged to this genealogy.

Who on earth would not want to be born as a descendant of Jesus Christ and belong to his genealogy? In the opposite way, none of us want to be born as a descendant of Adam and belong to his genealogy. The problem is that no one can choose his or her genealogy in the same way that none of us could choose our parents and families when we were born.

The Genealogy of Disobedience

If a person cannot choose to which genealogy he or she belongs, then who decides our genealogy? To know this, we need to reexamine the story of the first man God created. As I mentioned above, God created Adam, the first man. And God also made and gave him his wife Eve. Because God provided every resource in order to live happily in the Garden of Eden, Adam and Eve had many happy days.

God gave them the secret how to maintain happiness continually. What is the secret? They had to acknowledge God as their Creator and Lord and accept the fact that they were his creatures. In other words, they needed to maintain the right relationship with God. Adam and Eve lived in a dual relationship. They needed to keep their relationship with God on the upper level and to keep their husband and wife relationship with each other on the lower level.

Unless Adam and Eve maintained their husband and wife relationship well, they could not help destroying their happiness. For example, if Adam ignored his wife Eve or Eve deceived her husband Adam, their love relationship would be fractured and their happiness would ultimately be broken. Likewise, if they had a crack in their relationship with God, they could not enjoy a happy life and everything God allowed.

God gave Adam and Eve the way to acknowledges God as their Creator in a commandment: "The tree of the knowledge of good and evil, thou shalt not eat of it" (Gen 2:17, KJV). Why is the fruit of the tree of the knowledge of good and evil the way to acknowledge God as Creator?

The reason is simple. God himself is the final judge of good and evil. This commandment implies that man should not underestimate God's sovereignty.

This commandment is God's expression of protection and love for man—the request that man enjoy happiness under the wings of God's love. This commandment is also the expectation that people should acknowledge God as Creator. It was also a promise that a man can enjoy God's provision. God deeply loved Adam and Eve, and so he asked them, "you must not eat from the tree of the knowledge of good and evil" (Gen 2:17, NIV).

However, there is a fact that all of us know: human greed is unlimited. In spite of their abundant happiness, Adam and Eve wanted to escape from the status of mere creature. So when they had the chance, they ate of the tree of the knowledge of good and evil. They took God's warning "when you eat of it you will surely die" lightly or ignored it. If they had not done so, how could they dare to eat of it?

As I mentioned before, when God created Adam, God placed the Holy Spirit inside him. However, when Adam and Eve ate the prohibited fruit, the Holy Spirit left them. They became spiritually dead. Since then, all of the children Adam and Eve produced were born without the Spirit. Although they were born in flesh, they were spiritually dead. We are the same. We were born into the state of spiritual death when we were born into this world.

What is the form of spiritual death? In the upper level, people live saying there is no God. In the lower level, one's self-benefit becomes the only purpose for life. Others exist for his or her profit. In short, they live a self-centered life. And if one's life does not produce the desired results, he or she is usually painful and lonely, and sometimes desperate. Sometimes they hate others. Sometimes they boast. In a word, we are in the genealogy of Adam.

The Genealogy of Obedience

Every person is a descendant of Adam and Eve, including us. Consequently, our names are in the genealogy of death. This is not our choice—it is our destiny already determined when we were born. Some say it is too unfair because they think they did not sin at all.

God provided the genealogy of Jesus Christ that can be chosen by those who feel that belonging to the genealogy of death is unfair. Jesus Christ, first of all, wanted to remove the names from the genealogy of Adam and put them into the new genealogy. To do so, there was no other way but to make another genealogy.

That is why Jesus Christ became the last Adam. To end the genealogy of Adam, he could not help becoming the last Adam. Jesus became the last Adam by taking responsibility for Adam's, and his descendants', disobedience to God. Jesus Christ accepted the condemnation just as if he had disobeyed God. The result was death on the cross.

The reason Jesus Christ died on the cross was not because of disobedience, even though he was judged, and died as if he participated in the disobedience of Adam and his descendants. If the death of Jesus was the end of the story, the new genealogy could not have been made. However, God raised Jesus Christ three days after he died. The reason his resurrection is the beginning of the new genealogy is very simple. Jesus was resurrected! For the first time in human history, Someone, Jesus, offered hope to those who face death.

The Bible tells us that the resurrection of Jesus Christ—the last Adam—is the beginning of the new genealogy: "The first man Adam was made a living soul; the last Adam was made a quickening spirit" (1 Cor 15:45). This means that the first Adam had to die because he was made of soil, but because the last Adam Jesus Christ was born and resurrected by the Holy Spirit, he can make us descendants of Adam that are alive in spirit. In other words, we can be resurrected and enjoy eternal life.

The Bible contrasts the first Adam and the last Adam by saying, "For as by one man's disobedience many were made sinners, so by the obedience of one shall many be made righteous" (Rom 5:19). Here, the phrase "by one man's disobedience" indicates the disobedience of the first Adam. As a result of that, "as...many were made sinners" means that all people become sinners and die like Adam, because their names were written in the genealogy of Adam.

On the contrary, "by the obedience of one" indicates the obedience of the last Adam, Jesus Christ. Here, obedience means that he died on the cross for all descendants of Adam. Additionally, his death was not coerced, but voluntary. As a result, he rose again from the dead on the third day. The phrase, "Shall many be made righteous" means he forgives those who believe in the resurrected Jesus Christ and writes their names in his genealogy.

My Genealogy

All of us were born into this world as descendants of Adam. Our names were written on the genealogy of Adam from birth. This is unfair in each person's view because it is not the result of our sins and is not our choice as well. Nevertheless, we do not need to become desperate or complain because God personally gives us an equal opportunity to choose our destiny or genealogy.

Just as Adam determined our destinies through his disobedience to God even before we existed, Jesus Christ obeyed God even before we existed. He died tearing his flesh and pouring out his blood on the cross even before we were aware of his sacrifice. And that is not all! He rose again from the dead on the third day, creating a new genealogy—the genealogy of Jesus Christ and that of the last Adam at the same time.

The genealogy of Jesus is also the genealogy of life. If our names are written on this genealogy of life, we do not really die. How is this possible? Even if our bodies die, we will be resurrected and enter into the eternal life that God gives. We will enjoy that eternal life where God is: in heaven. However, if we desire to remain in the genealogy of Adam, that is also our choice. Surely, we should enter the genealogy of Jesus Christ. It depends upon our personal choice. Which genealogy will you choose, the genealogy of life or death?

Chapter 11

From Defeat to Victory

"An account of the genealogy of Jesus the Messiah, the son of David, the son of Abraham" (Matthew 1:1, NRSV).

Christians are people who consider Jesus Christ as their Lord and Savior. In other words, they are people whose sins have been forgiven because of the precious blood that Jesus shed on the Cross. Not only have their sins been forgiven when Jesus Christ came into their hearts, but also the Holy Spirit came into them. To express it differently, they have been reborn. That is not all. They became sons and daughters of God. As a result their lives have been changed. They have tasted joy and peace. They have new hobbies and friends.

Now Christians can read the Bible and pray. On top of it, they are now excited about attending worship services. Can these transformed Christians be devoid of hardships? Not at all! Christians can have problems! For example, their families and relatives can misunderstand them or persecute them. However, the biggest cause of problems for Christians comes from themselves. What is the cause of the problems? That is simple. There are two kinds of natures inside of a Christian; one is the nature that desires to live according to God's will and another according to their own will. The two natures always fight with each other. The evidence that a Christian has two kinds of nature is a proof that he or she is truly reborn.

The same goes true with Abraham, David, and Jesus Christ. Although these three people are the greatest believers written at the front of New Testament, they also had two kinds of nature for they were the same human beings as we are. They had the earnest hope to live according to the will of God, but at the same time, they had strong urges to manage their lives according to whatever they wanted. At normal times, they were heroes who lived according to the will of God, but at other times, they wanted to live according to their sinful nature. In fact Abraham and David tasted the bitter cup of temptation because of such desires. They fell many times to such temptations and failed miserably at such times. One of the reasons they became heroes is that they did not stay fallen, drenched with failure, but rose again, trusting God.

Abraham from Defeat to Victory

Abraham is called the "Father of Faith." When God told him to "Leave your country, your people and your father's household" in Genesis 12:1, he did not hesitate to leave. What a man of will power! That is not all. When God told him to sacrifice his only son, he decided to obey God's command (Gen 22:9-10). Abraham was a great believer who possessed true faith and obedience.

Do not be dismayed! Even Abraham had numerous temptations and failures. In other words, he was a human being like us. If so, what kind of temptations and failures did Abraham have? First, he disobeyed God's command that he should leave his relatives, and took his nephew Lot with him. This may not look serious at first glance, but it was a shrewd manipulation of God's word. Despite God's promise in Genesis 12:2, "I will make you into a great nation," Abraham tried to accomplish God's word through a human method, his nephew.

Second, to save his life, Abraham introduced his wife as his sister, not once, but twice! Once, he went down to Egypt with his wife to survive a famine. Listen to his cunning words in Genesis 12:11-13: "As he was about to enter Egypt, he said to his wife Sarai, "I know what a beautiful woman you are. When the Egyptians see you, they will say, `This is his wife.' Then they will kill me but will let you live. Say you are my sister, so that I will be treated well for your sake and my life will be spared because of you." He was an opportunist who was willing to risk his wife's safety to preserve his own life. The second time he did that was when he was living temporarily in the region of Gerar (Gen 20:2). If God had not intervened both times, Abraham would have lost his wife. If he were to live in Korea right now, he would be driven out of the house by his wife. Who can live with such a man as husband?

Third, Abraham took Hagar as a concubine according to Genesis 16:3. Of course, men at that time could take concubines upon the approval of their wives. It was a justifiable custom especially when a woman could not bear a son. Since Sarah the wife of Abraham could not have a baby, she gave Hagar to her husband. It might have been due to her hope that Abraham could get a son through Hagar according to

Genesis 16:2-3. However, having Hagar as a concubine was a serious problem. Abraham tried to fulfill God's promise with a strictly human method. God already gave Abraham the following promise: "The word of the LORD came to him: A son coming from your own body will be your heir. He took him outside and said, "Look up at the heavens and count the stars -- if indeed you can count them." Then he said to him, "So shall your offspring be" (Gen 15:4-5).

David from Defeat to Victory

David was a great king that made Israel, which had become very weak, into a strong nation. The great king united a divided Israel. By trusting God, David the man of faith killed beasts and won against a formidable Philistine foe, Goliath. He wrote poems of Psalm after appreciating the heart of God. A lot of people all over the world have received consolation and encouragement when reading and meditating on the Psalms. Truly David was a great man spiritually, politically and militarily. We can become a great warrior of faith like him.

When we look at David who failed after yielding to temptation, we can have hope even if we fail. If so, what kind of failure did David have? First, David lost against the battle of sexual temptation. His army was in battle for the country. At that time, David was not where he should have been, doing something he should not have been doing when he saw Bathsheba, whose husband was in the battlefield. Lust turned to covetousness in David and took her by the power of his kingship, according to 2 Samuel 11:4. Uriah, the husband of Bathsheba, was one of David's beloved generals. Moreover, Uriah was the type of general who did not lack in devotion and loyalty to David and his country. But David did not resist the temptation of sexual desire and took her by force. Faith that he had accumulated collapsed at once. He not only betrayed God, but also lost the faith of a subordinate who had committed his life to David.

The second incident was spawned from the first. Fear and adultery now accused David and tempted him to commit murder. He gave in to their siren voices. After learning that Bathsheba had conceived, he used all kinds of measures to conceal the incident. He gave Uriah special vacation. He made Uriah drunk. It was to make him sleep with his wife. After each method failed, David sent a confidential letter to Joab, embroiling him in his sin, to have Uriah killed by the enemy's sword (2 Sam 11:17).

Third, temptation and defeat stalked David in the problem with one of his sons. Among his many sons, Absalom was his favorite, treated with special privilege. Part of the reason was on account of his outstanding outward appearance. Listen to the description of Absalom: "In all Israel there was not a man so highly praised for his handsome appearance as Absalom. From the top of his head to the sole of his foot there was no blemish in him (2 Sam 14:25)." Due to this reason, David had favoritism on Absalom. Out of rage against Amnon who raped his sister, Absalom killed Amnon (2 Sam 13:28-29). David not only generously forgave his son, but also honored him. Afterwards, Absalom rebelled against his father David and took his wives, but still David did not kill Absalom because of favoritism. David had to flee Jerusalem to escape the rebellious army of Absalom. In short, David committed a spiritual "crime" that he could not raise his son in faith and character because of his sin of favoritism.

Jesus Christ from Defeat to Victory

Jesus Christ was the greatest person in history. He was born of a virgin. Without a formal academic education, he taught the Sermon on the Mount, the greatest teaching in human history. He also performed many miracles. He opened the eyes of blind people, healed lepers and drove demons out of people. Not only that, he raised people from the dead. He was the Messiah who finally died on the cross for mankind and was resurrected.

In spite of all that, Jesus Christ was a human like us. He had many temptations. After fasting forty days, he was tempted to misuse his miraculous power selfishly on food. The devil also tempted him by offering him all the power and glory of the earth, if he would bow down to the devil. Jesus was also tempted to be acclaimed as the highest religious leader by those who came to worship by plunging himself from the top of the temple and landing safely on the ground (Lk 4:1-13, Mt 4:1-11).

His greatest temptation was the fight in Gethsemane. Jesus, right before dying on the cross, fought a gruesome battle through prayer at the crossroad between life and death, defeat or victory. He prayed like this: "My Father, if it is possible, may this cup be taken from me. Yet not as I will, but as you will," according to Matthew 26:39. But the reason why Jesus Christ had to come to this world was to fulfill the will of God. The book of Hebrews describes Jesus Christ, who came only to fulfill the will of God, like this: "Then I said, 'Here I am -- it is written about me in the scroll -- I have come to do your will, O God'" (Heb 10:7). By this reason, fighting the gruesome fight on his knees in Gethsemane, he avoided defeat and finished in victory with, "Yet not as I will, but as you will"

(Mt 26:39). Jesus Christ was fully human and fully God at the same time. Since he was fully human, he had to face all the temptations that we have. However, when Jesus relied upon His relationship with the Father and drew on the power of the Holy Spirit, He overcame all the temptations. Because He was also God, he could save us from our sins. If he was not both fully God and human, how could he save us who fall into sins?

This is the difference between Jesus Christ from Abraham and David. The author of Hebrews describes Jesus Christ as following: "For we do not have a high priest who is unable to sympathize with our weaknesses, but we have one who has been tempted in every way, just as we are -- yet was without sin" (Heb 4:15). Since he received all the temptations by himself, he can sympathize with us when we are exposed and fall under temptations. In other words, he understands us and is ready to help us.

I from Defeat to Victory

What kind of lessons can we learn from the temptations that Abraham and David faced? We can get following three lessons. The first lesson is that, like Abraham, David and Jesus, we are subject to temptations anytime and anywhere.

As I discussed in the introduction, if we are truly reborn, we will have two kinds of nature: the nature to follow the will of God and the nature to choose our own will. The apostle Paul vividly describes two kinds of nature that he experienced like this: "For the sinful nature desires what is contrary to the Spirit, and the Spirit desires what is contrary to the sinful nature. They are in conflict with each other, so that you do not do what you want," according to Galatians 5:17.

This Bible verse tells that trials and temptations that we sometimes experience are ultimately a fight against ourselves. It may look like the trial is due to circumstance. It may look like the trial originates from other people. But, the trial is a fight against ourselves.

Look at Abraham. That he brought Lot with him was due to his greed. That he almost lost his wife twice was not due to the circumstances. He, himself, chose to refer to his wife as his sister. Did his wife force Abraham to take Hagar as a concubine? Not at all! He wanted it that way. He employed a human method in order to satisfy his strong passion to fulfill his fleshly desire.

Look at David! Taking Bathsheba and killing her husband, Uriah, is all due to his desire to fulfill his own lust. The reason why he was too charitable to his son Absalom could have been due to the fatherly love, but at a deeper level, he considered his own law more important than

God's law. What was the result? Because of the son, not only David had to flee for his life, but the whole nation was plunged into war.

Therefore, when we are facing a temptation, we can actively say that we are confirming we are reborn. However, we have to acknowledge that we have to look for the cause of temptation not only from without, but *within*. In other words, we have to look into our fleshly desires that have not been subdued. Whenever we are facing trials and temptations, we should not attribute them to other people or environments, but to ourselves. When we take responsibility for them, then we can finally find a solution to the problem.

The second lesson that we get from temptations is that we change little by little to a hero of faith. Abraham and David did not become the heroes of faith at the moment when they were called by God. They became men of faith through many trials. In that sense, trials and temptations are necessary to us Christians. Temptations to do evil expose our weaknesses and reveal our need for God, so that through them our faith grows.

Look at Abraham. He failed three times to big temptations and tasted defeat. However, out of temptations and defeats, Abraham could come to the place that he could surrender his will to God's will. Look at the last step of his blossoming faith. When God ordered Abraham to sacrifice Isaac as a burnt offering, he did not complain, nor make an argument. He was silent and accepted the will of God. As the result, he became the father of faith.

Look at David. He, too, fell miserably to temptations three times and tasted serious defeat. What did he learn from his failures? It was sincere repentance. Being a king, he could have hidden the problem to the end. However, he repented honestly of his problem in front of God and his men. Thorough repentance means that one becomes humble. David was a man who ascended to the highest position that a man could ever reach, but when repenting, he went as low as he could go.

The same is true for us. We frequently fall into temptations that we do not wish or seek. When that happens, let us not excuse or defend ourselves. Let us be humble in front of God and other spiritual Christians. We need to repent. Of course, pain accompanies repentance . However, without such a process, we cannot be transformed into heroes of faith. The greatest Christians are those who experienced full repentance.

The third lesson is concerning the importance of prayer. In spite of being the God-man, Jesus Christ prayed when tempted. Without the prayer of Gethsemane, he would not have successfully carried out redemption on the cross. That sorrowful prayer! The prayer that turned tear drops into blood! This kind of prayer enabled Jesus Christ to overcome the last temptation. The same is true for us. Trials and temptations are always hovering around us: "Our enemy the devil prowls around like a roaring lion looking for someone to devour" (1 Pet 5:8). Through prayer we come to the cross every day. We have to crucify ourselves through prayer. We can overcome temptations only when we do that. We can taste the victory of resurrection only when we do that. When we pray like this God hears our prayers. When we pray like this, Father God and Jesus Christ will carry the temptation on behalf of us. When we pray like this, the Holy Spirit comes to us and strengthens us. He gives us abilities. He will make us victors against all temptations. God the Father, Jesus Christ the son, and the Holy Spirit will work in and for us so that we can have blessed lives as victors.

Chapter 12

God's Person

"An account of the genealogy of Jesus the Messiah, the son of David, the son of Abraham." (Matthew 1:1)

God has been looking for people from the beginning. Why is God looking for people? The reason is simple. God wants to build the kingdom of God on the earth through them. For this definite purpose, God created humankind based on his image. Then God said to them: "... Be fruitful and multiply, and fill the earth and subdue it ... have domination over ... every living thing that moves upon the earth" (Gen 1:28). This was an invitation for humans to build God's kingdom on the earth. Was this request of God accomplished by Adam and Eve? No, they left God because of their egotism and arrogance. After Adam and Eve disobeyed God's commandment and sinned, all people have not been concerned about what God wants. Their lives are separated from God. Nevertheless, God has never given up building his kingdom on the earth through people.

How does God construct his kingdom on the earth through people? What kind of person will he use for building his kingdom? Will he use the intelligent, the rich, or the religious persons? Those are not God's determinative qualities for the work. God can call them for his purpose, but first and foremost, God looks for those after his own heart.

In Scripture, it is impossible to find one who fully comprehends God's mind. Even though Abraham and David were described as people of God in Matthew 1:1, they were not God's persons from the beginning of their lives. They also were human like us. When they were called by God as his workers, they had a lot of obstacles to overcome in order to be fit for the mission as God's person. Even Jesus, who was truly human, had things to learn, but he did not sin in the process.

God has not called flawless people to accomplish his purpose on the earth. Moreover, no one has reached flawlessness on the earth. God has called those who are weak and insufficient, prepared and trained them as God's people to build his kingdom on the earth, and sent them to those who have never heard the gospel. If this is the case, how did God discipline Abraham, David, and Jesus in order to prepare and train them as his people for His work?

Abraham as God's Person

First of all, let us look at Abraham's life. When God called him, he was not really mature enough to be named as God's person. He did not ask what God wanted him to do. Rather, he struggled without God's guidance to accomplish God's promise which was to "make of you a great nation" (Gen 12:2). As a result, he experienced failure. At that time, God trained him through diverse experiences of "separation," even from his relatives, in order to make him the father of the people of God.

The first separation of Abraham was from Lot, who was a special nephew. Lot was a son of his younger brother who died. Abraham loved his nephew in particular because he did not have a son. That is why Abraham brought Lot to Canaan even though God was against Abraham's decision. However, God used Abraham and Lot's quarrels over possessions to train Abraham. After leaving his special nephew, Abraham had felt a sense of futility and of frustration beyond description. At that time, he came to God and asked, "What Shall I do?" The back of Genesis says, "The LORD said to Abraham, after Lot had separated from him ..." (Gen 13:14). Finally, Abraham was ready to listen to God after his nephew was gone.

The second separation of Abraham was from his wife who possessed outstanding beauty. Abraham and his wife were not only a married couple and a partner with the same purpose (Heb 11:16), had also relied on one another in childlessness. However, when Abraham struggled to save himself from an Egyptian king, he was taken away from his beautiful wife (Gen 12:15, 20:2). Of course, through God's intervention, he drew out his wife from the king, but the sadness of being separated from his wife was very heavy. Through this experience, he was disciplined to be named with the people of God.

The final separation Abraham experienced was from Ishmael, who was highly valued for thirteen years. Although Ishmael was a child of Abraham's concubine, he was Abraham's son by blood. Over time, Abraham forgot about God as he was hooked on Ishmael as the child of promise. As a result, God could not call Abraham to fulfill his purpose.

When he, eventually, had to be separated from Ishmael, it was "very distressing" (Gen 21:11). It was an especially sorrowful time for Abraham. Nevertheless, if the separation had not taken place, then Abraham might not have been God's person.

David as God's Person

Now we turn to look at King David's journey to become part of the people of God. His life was full of "losing." The words of "separating" and "losing" have a similar meaning, however, there are considerable differences. Since losing includes separation through death, meaning of separation is subordinated to the concept of losing. David became part of the people of God through more adversity than Abraham.

David's first experience with losing is Jonathan. When David lost his best friend, he sang that their relationship was more intimate than love between female and male (2 Sam 1:26). This is proof of their close relationship. The depth of their relationship was revealed when David was threatened by Saul, Jonathan's father. In spite of the danger, Jonathan saved David, from the evil scheme of his father. His motive was, undoubtedly, based on this special friendship. In 1 Samuel, Jonathan's love toward David was expressed like this: "Jonathan made David swear again by his love for him; for he loved him as he loved his own life" (1 Sam 20:17). Thus, when he lost Jonathan, his best friend, his sadness was the greatest. However, through losing his loving friend, he was learning to love God more.

David's second loss was his baby who was born to Bathsheba. While the baby had a serious illness, David prayed to God and fasted for a week. He was the king of a country, but he bowed before God, the Lord of life. The innocent baby died (2 Sam 12:15-18), but through this process, David realized how to love only God.

Finally, David lost his son Absalom, which had a different meaning for David than the death of his baby. David loved Absalom even more than his other sons. Thus, since Absalom was David's favorite, David did not punish him when he killed his brother, Amnon. In the end, David, as he fled for his life, was separated from Absalom.

2 Samuel describes David's partiality: "The heart of the king went out, yearning for Absalom …" (2 Sam 13:39). Even though Absalom rose up against and was killed in the process, David cried out deeply and said, "O my son Absalom, my son, my son Absalom! Would that I had died instead of you, O Absalom, my son, my son." (2 Sam 18:33) Through this process, David was disciplined to be God's person.

Jesus Christ as God's Person

Finally, let us look at the life of Jesus Christ. Jesus is different from Abraham and David. In that, he had divine nature as well as humanity, but Abraham and David were just human. Moreover, Jesus was different in another ways. In order to become God's person, Abraham had to be separated from those who were precious to him; David had to lose those he loved; but Jesus had to give up himself and be recognized as the Son of God through the cross. But what did Jesus give up in order to live with mankind? First, he had to leave the glory of heaven. Jesus had been with the Father forever, and the Holy Spirit before the beginning of the world. However, Jesus Christ laid aside His glory. He prayed for the glory: "So now, Father, glorify me in your own presence with the glory that I had in your presence before the world existed" (Jn 17:5).

Second, he had to give up the status of being called God's son. He carried away mankind's sin through suffering on the cross, and God turned away. It is evident or clear that Jesus gave up his status as God's son, in Mark it states, "Darkness came over the whole land" (Mk 15:33) and "At three o'clock Jesus cried out with a loud voice, 'Eloi, Eloi, lema sabachthani?' which means, 'My God, my God, why have you forsaken me?'" (Mk 15:34). If Jesus Christ had not abandoned himself in this way, how could he become the Savior who forgives sinners?

Third he had to abandon his life, the way of the cross brought death. However, the fact that Jesus did not give up his life by himself is evident in two places. John records that he died earlier than the two robbers (Jn 19:33), as it was no longer necessary to suffer further on the cross since He had purged of sins of humanity. In addition, Hebrews records that Jesus Christ already knew how miserable he would be dying on the cross. He predicted his death where. He explained: "I lay down my life for the sheep" (Jn 10:15). Jesus Christ abandoned his life by himself for our sins (Heb 2:9). He was God's person for the mission.

I as God's Person

Abraham, David, and Jesus were not ready from birth for God's mission. When God first called them for his purpose, they needed discipline to be God's person. When they responded to God's calling, they expected God's physical blessing, but, God did not fill their expectation. Instead of material and visual blessing, God disciplined them to make them ready to be with Him forever and to achieve God's mission on earth. God's concerns are not in giving material possession or fame to humanity, but making us the people of God.

It could be said that these may be important exemplars for those who want to become people of God. We must first learn experience "separation" from all lesser loyalties in becoming God's person and a part of the people of God. Abraham became a part of the people of God through a process of diverse separations from those with whom he had physical affinity such as Lot, Sarah, and Ishmael. Likewise, if we do not separate ourselves from the possessions that we have, we cannot become the person God desires, nor belong to the people of God.

But, what do we need to be separated from? First of all, it may be people. Have you experienced separation from close people such as families, best friends, or faithful partners in some cases because of your commitment to Christ, or because you were attached more to them than to Christ? It is likely that you have experienced separations in your life. In many cases, you have been trained through the process of separation to become God's person and part of the people of God.

It is important to note that separating does not limit people, and sometimes can be healthy. When we are crying out to God because of weakness, we might become closer to God. Separating from material possession may cause great sadness, but when we seriously pray to God, he touches us in his mercy. Thus, if we surrender before God's intention, we are slowly becoming God's person and a true part of the people of God.

Second we must learn that we can experience "losing" just as David did in order to become God's person. David lost those he loved such as Jonathan—his best friend—a baby who was born by his lovely wife, Bathsheba, and Absalom, a grown son who was this favorite. In "losing" experiences, what did David realize? He realized that physical love has limitations, but God's love is forever.

David experienced "gaining" through "losing." In other words, although he lost his physical loved ones, he finally realized God's love. As a result, he became part of the people of God. Similarly, we cannot become God's people having all that we want. The apostle Paul says, "Dying is gain" (Phil 1:21).

Third we must learn that we might experience "abandonment" just as Jesus did. Since he gave up the glory of heaven, he was able to carry out his life and work on earth in faithfulness. In John, Jesus' prayer was filled with glory: "I glorified you on earth by finishing the work that you gave me to do. So now, Father, glorify me in your own presence with the glory that I had in your presence before the world existed" (Jn 17:4-5).

Jesus Christ gave up his status as God's son as well as his life. As a result, he "was declared to be Son of God with power according to the spirit of holiness by the resurrection from the dead (Rom 1:4)," and has become the Savior of humankind. In the same manner, we must give up the blessing of material possessions or fame to become God's person and to be a part of the people of God. Ultimately, we must abandon ourselves, giving up our ego. Apart from abandoning our ego, we cannot be changed to be God's person to fulfill God's calling for us on earth or even be a final part of the people of God.

Chapter 13

Melchizedek

"An account of the genealogy of Jesus the Messiah, the son of David, the son of Abraham" (Matthew 1:1, NRSV).

Several Biblical figures elude ready understanding; Melchizedek is one of them. His name appears in the entire Bible only three times: Genesis, Psalm, and Hebrews. Every time he was mentioned, Melchizedek is related to Abraham, David, and Jesus whose names open the book of Matthew.

The question arises: who is Melchizedek and what did he do? According to the Bible, He was a high priest. The duty of priests is to mediate between God and man. It is recorded that Melchizedek mediated for Abraham. David sang about the mediating role of Melchizedek. The writer of the book of Hebrews explained Jesus' ministry by comparing it with Melchizedek's life.

These connections bind Abraham, David, and Jesus -- who appear in Matthew 1:1-- to Melchizedek in several ways that we shall explore here. First, we shall observe the Biblical introduction of Melchizedek in Genesis, Psalm, and Hebrews. Next we will correlate the relationship of Abraham, David, and Jesus to Melchizedek.

Abraham and Melchizedek

Genesis 14:17-20 introduces us to Melchizedek and allows us to understand Melchizedek as one of prerequisites to understand Abraham. "After his return from the defeat of Chedorlaomer and the kings who were with him, the king of Sodom went out to meet him at the Valley of Shaveh (that is, the King's Valley). And King Melchizedek of Salem brought out bread and wine; he was priest of God Most High. He blessed him and said, *"Blessed be Abram by God Most High, maker of heaven and earth; and blessed be God Most High, who has delivered your enemies into your hand... And Abram gave him one tenth of everything."*

The background of this story is well known to us, having been taught the story of Abraham in Sunday school. In review: four allied Babylonian nations invaded Abraham's nephew, Lot's, city of residence and looted the town. Upon hearing the news, Abraham attacked the Babylonian alliance with 318 soldiers whom he had personally trained, to save Lot and his properties. On Abraham's journey home, Melchizedek met, received, and blessed Abraham.

Who is Melchizedek? First, he is introduced as a King of Salem, which means a king of peace (Heb 7:2). King Melchizedek offered bread and wine to Abraham and his men, who were very tired after battle. From this act, we can draw that Melchizedek is a king of peace: to physiologically and emotionally tired and thirsty soldiers, bread and wine means much more than it would appear. The bread and wine takes on a metaphoric and spiritual significance.

Secondly, Melchizedek is a king of righteousness. According to Hebrew language, Melchizedek is a combination of two words, Melchi and Sedek. Melchi means a king and Sedek means righteousness (Heb 7:2). Because he blessed Abraham, we conclude that Melchizedek considered Abraham's efforts to save Lot and his property to be righteous.

Finally, Melchizedek is introduced as "priest of God Most High." A priest is defined as a vocation whose mission is to deliver God's messages to ordinary people. Because God is the Most High, only properly prepared priests can receive God's message. That day, God's message to Abraham came through Melchizedek. First, he prayed for Abraham's prosperity because Abraham performed a righteous effort, fit for God's intention and plan.

The second message was that Abraham only won the battle as a direct result of God's help. Even though Abraham had trained his soldiers and attacked the Babylonian alliance at night, without God's help, Abraham could not have succeeded. God's blessing indicates divine protection of Abraham, and asks that Abraham render glory and honor where the glory and honor was due. In response to being made aware of God's help, Abraham rendered a tenth of his regained property and loot as an offering to God through his priest Melchizedek.

David and Melchizedek

Psalm 110 helps us to understand the relationship of Melchizedek to David:

The LORD says to my lord, 'Sit at my right hand until I make your enemies your footstool...The LORD sends out from Zion your mighty scepter. Rule in the midst of your foes. Your people will offer themselves willingly on the day you lead your forces on the holy mountains. From the womb of the morning, like dew, your youth will come to you. The LORD has sworn and will not change his mind...You are a priest forever according to the order of Melchizedek.' The Lord is at your right hand; he will shatter kings on the day of his wrath. He will execute judgment among the nations, filling them with corpses; he will shatter heads over the wide earth. He will drink from the stream by the path; therefore he will lift up his head (vv 1-7).

When David wrote the book of Psalm, he was unaware that he was the bridge between the past and the future: Melchizedek, who blessed Abraham in Genesis 14, and Jesus Christ the High Priest. In other words, David, who inherited Melchizedek's role is the bridge between Melchizedek, who met Abraham; and Jesus Christ, who became the High Priest. This part of Psalms contains three primary points. First, the Lord of David is the King. The Lord holds the scepter of the King and ruled. The People of the King offer themselves readily, and accept the King's governance. Let us examine verses 2 and 3 once again: *"The LORD sends out from Zion your mighty scepter. Rule in the midst of your foes. Your people will offer themselves willingly on the day you lead your forces on the holy mountains. From the womb of the morning, like dew, your youth will come to you."*

Secondly, the Lord of David is the High Priest. Let us review verses 1 and 4 once again: *"The LORD says to my lord, "Sit at my right hand until I make your enemies your footstool. The LORD has sworn and will not change his mind, "You are a priest forever according to the order of Melchizedek."* The Lord of David is the High Priest who sits on the right side of God and prays for people.

Finally, the Lord of David is the Judge. Let us inspect verses 5 and 6 once again: *"The Lord is at your right hand; he will shatter kings on the day of his wrath. He will execute judgment among the nations, filling them with corpses; he will shatter heads over the wide earth."* According to these verses, when David's Lord finishes sitting on the right side of God and praying for people, he will judge all nations.

According to this Psalm, David's Lord is the High Priest and the Judge of all nations. Melchizedek was the first in the line of men who held that august status of duality, as bestowed by the LORD: Melchizedek was both a king and a high priest. David described his Lord as both the King and the High Priest by comparing the Lord with Melchizedek. Through inference, we determine that the Lord of David is the anticipated Messiah: Jesus Christ.

Jesus Christ and Melchizedek

Hebrews 5 aids us in discovering Melchizedek's connection to Jesus Christ:

> So also Christ did not glorify himself in becoming a high priest, but was appointed by the one who said to him, 'You are my Son, today I have begotten you' as he says also in another place, 'You are a priest forever, according to the order of Melchizedek.' In the days of his flesh, Jesus offered up prayers and supplications, with loud cries and tears, to the one who was able to save him from death, and he was heard because of his reverent submission. Although he was a Son, he learned obedience through what he suffered; and having been made perfect, he became the source of eternal salvation for all who obey him, having been designated by God a high priest according to the order of Melchizedek (vv 5-10).

Jesus Christ is the prophet, priest, and king. He proclaims the gospel of salvation and sits as eternal judge as the prophet and the king. He prays for Christians, while sitting on the right hand of God as the priest. Therefore, Jesus Christ is both the king and the priest. His dual status is parallel to Melchizedek's similar dual status. In fact, one could make the analogy that Melchizedek's status is a metaphoric precursor to that of Jesus.

However, Jesus Christ is introduced in Hebrews 5 just as the priest. A priest, as the Old Testament shows, understands that people are ignorant and easy to be wayward (Heb 5:2). Jesus Christ qualifies for the requirements because he was also wholly man with human finiteness, giving up all glories in heaven. Hebrews 5:5 describes Jesus: *"You are my Son, today I have begotten you."* In other words, Jesus was perfectly capable to fulfill the role as priest who can pray for and mediate on behalf of fallen humanity, for though being nothing in himself and having emptied himself and taken on flesh, was everything in God.

Christ's vocation, bestowed by God's call is that of a priest (v 4). The book of Hebrews mentions God's calling for Jesus in this way: *"You are a priest forever, according to the order of Melchizedek"* (v 6). As earlier indicated, Melchizedek was the priest who blessed Abraham, and he was mentioned as a metaphor for the priest of the future about whom David proclaimed. Jesus Christ was present in the priestly blessing of Abraham and the one about whom David prophesied, Melchizedek.

Jesus Christ has two requirements to be a priest. One is the Old Testament requirements. However, none of priests in the Old Testament could be the eternal priest because all died and their status as priests ended with death. Jesus needed to have another requirement above and beyond that of the other priests in the Old Testament in order to be the eternal priest about whom David had prophesied.

According to Hebrews 5, Jesus' unique qualification to be the eternal priest whom other priests had not experienced was his perseverance, and Passion. His suffering in the Passion events was so tremendous; His tears and agony demonstrate the painfulness of his suffering (v 7). Jesus "through what he suffered... having been designated by God a high priest according to the order of Melchizedek" (vv 8-10).

"Me" and Melchizedek

We have briefly reviewed the mysterious figure, Melchizedek who appears in the Bible only three times. His life is difficult to understand. The writer of the book of Hebrews agreed by saying *"About this we have much to say that is hard to explain, since you have become dull in understanding"* (Heb 5:11). Melchizedek is a figure about whom all have difficulty in understanding.

However, one fact is that Melchizedek was a priest. First, he was a priest who blessed Abraham. Second, he was a priest about whom David had prophesied. Finally, Jesus Christ was the high priest as Melchizedek had been. As a result, Melchizedek paralleled with Jesus who, on the right side of God, continually prays for us.

Jesus Christ was anointed to be the priest and has greatly impacted our lives. The Holy Spirit came into our lives and cleansed our hearts when we were forgiven and accepted Him as our savior. In other words, we are also anointed as priests (1 Jn 2:20). Peter called us priests like kings (1 Pet 2:9). John mentioned twice that God takes us as kings (Rev 1:6, 5:10).

We, as priests, should follow Melchizedek's life in three different manners. First, we should pray for each other to be blessed as Melchizedek blessed Abraham. We, sometimes, are misunderstood and are persecuted while we attempt to live in the way Christians should live. As Melchizedek blessed Abraham who came from battlefield, we should pray for and bless each other, especially those who are tired and exhausted.

As Melchizedek offered bread and wine to fatigued Abraham, we as priests should meet others' particular needs. Though it is important to pray for others, it is also necessary to meet their physical needs in addition to the spiritual. Otherwise, we cannot be called as priests. James describes the role of priests in this way: *"If a brother or sister is ill-clad and in lack of daily food, and one of you says to them, 'Go in peace, be warmed and filled,' without giving them the things needed for the body, what does it profit? So faith by itself, if it has no works, is dead*" (Jas 2:15-17).

Secondly, Melchizedek models our role as a priest who prays for us. David described Melchizedek as an eternal priest who prayed for others, sitting on the right side of God. We also should live in that way. As priests, we should pray for each other. The mark of a mature Christian is his selfless prayer for others. We should continually pray for others within our covenantal community. Then, we will be fulfilling our calling as priests and our community can grow strong and firm in the Lord.

Priests should not limit their prayer within the boundary of merely lifting up their church members. We should pray for our family members and friends. We should pray for people around us who have not received Jesus as their Savior. This form of prayer requires much perseverance and love. Moreover, we should pray for political leaders of our country. Our safety, security, and balance rely upon their wisdom, and guidance. Conversely, their mistakes will lead our country into difficulty and imbalance (1 Tim 2:2). Third, Melchizedek is our role model as a priest who endures and perseveres. Jesus also became the priest who followed Melchizedek's model and underwent tremendous difficulty and hardship. We must do likewise. Once we begin to pray for others, to share our time and resources, and to move toward great spiritual deepening, much difficulty will ensue. Though it is a privilege to pray for others, it is also difficult for us to endure; we should sacrifice what is precious to us on the altar, so that the smoke may glorify God, like the incense of the old temple.

I beseech you to share your time and resources. Only people who have shared their lives with others know how much this benefits us, yet requires great perseverance. Some people sacrifice their time and endeavors because they understand the pain of the world. Others sacrifice their properties, resources, and energies. However, it is only the people who share their lives with others that know the hidden recovery and power of the Lord, as he rejuvenates and empowers us to do his work.

Chapter 14

God's Mission

"An account of the genealogy of Jesus the Messiah, the son of David, the son of Abraham" (Matthew 1:1, NRSV).

God created man because he wanted to have fellowship with man that was based on love. That was visible through a lot of situations. God provided everything necessary before He created humans. The human pair could just rejoice and enjoy everything which God created. More than that! Afterwards, when the humans broke their fellowship with God, God still did not discard His love toward humanity.

As we know, the first humans, Adam and Eve, rejected God's great love. Adam and Eve abandoned God. But God's love for them was like an almost one-sided love, because He constantly loved those who left him. God showed his love again and again. He made garments of skins for them who were naked and clothed them (Gen 3:21). After that they greatly increased in number.

What is their response to God's love? They forsook his will. Man refused to worship God in his heart, and lived to practice every kind of sin. Later, God revealed his love for mankind through Noah and his family. In other words, He preserved righteous Noah and his family for the salvation of mankind (Gen 6:9), and God made mankind increase in number again through his family.

Did men admire such a love of God? Of course not. Instead, they turned against God. They built the Tower of Babel to compete against God (Gen 11:1-3). They decided to reject God's love. They rejected God by not spreading out over the earth. God's love for mankind was trampled down cruelly again. God still loved mankind so that they flourished, but He was rejected again and again.

Did God forsake mankind as a result? Of course not! God's one sided love for mankind became deeper. Like in the movie *Marathon*, where the mother loved, agonized over, and devoted more of her time to her sick son than even her healthy son, God still loved sick mankind and eagerly wanted to restore the fellowship with them. But as it is from Genesis 1 to 11, mankind demonstrated their wickedness.

From now on, God's love for mankind would come through another way. That was salvation through a Savior and restoration of fellowship. Instead of the method of direct salvation, God chose the method to send Savior for every mankind. As we know, God began to plan the way of salvation, the restoration of fellowship through the way that Savior died for all mankind on the cross.

Abraham's Mission

God has begun a new way to save for mankind starting with Abraham. God had a great purpose and called Abraham to be involved in it. God said to Abraham, "Leave your country, your people and your father's household and go to the land I will show you" (Gen 12:1). Already as I said, God called Abraham for mankind. For that purpose God spoke in this way "...And all people will be blessed through you" (Gen 12:3).

Also God promised a blessing for Abraham. Actually, God blessed him many times in his life. He had many possessions. He had many children. He enjoyed a long life of 175 years. He never had a major sickness, but lived healthy, and finally he passed all of his blessings on to his son.

All of the blessings that Abraham enjoyed were only temporary and earthly. God ultimately had a purpose to send a Savior into the world through Abraham's descendants. Through this Savior, God had a plan to save mankind. Although Abraham did not understand God's will completely, God called Abraham from the beginning for a world mission. Sure enough, God is the God of mission.

Abraham's life was a missionary life, whether he was conscious of it or not. How can we say that? We have several reasons.

First, Abraham left his home country and lived as a stranger in other lands. His country was Ur of the Chaldeans. But he left his country and followed God here and there as He told him to go. This part of his life was similar to any other missionary who has left a country and followed God.

Second, Abraham went from place to place to preach about God, both directly and indirectly. He arrived at Shechem and built an altar for God who had appeared to him. (Gen 12:7). His life of faith gained the attention of the people of Shechem who were accustomed of many gods to worship. This was a great life of witness as a missionary of these days going to an uncultivated land of the gospel and built a church.

Third, Abraham lived under God's special care and protection. Missionaries also experience this kind of care and protection. When he lost his wife in Gerar, God intervened and protected his wife. As a result Abraham could preach about God to the Gentiles indirectly (Gen 12:17, 20:13). Indeed Abraham prayed publicly for them in Gerar, and through God's answer, he could preach about God (Gen 20:17).

David's Mission

God called Abraham for salvation of mankind. With David, God displayed his purpose in the concrete. Is David a suitable person who had a vision for salvation of mankind? Of course not. He was only a country boy who was born in a small town, Bethlehem, but he grew in his understanding of God's mission in his life. He was excluded from his parents and his brothers. He was a shepherd boy who took care of some sheep. He was a true Jew who was prejudiced against the Gentiles.

However, not only did God make David a king of Israel, but also God gave him a great revelation that God would save mankind. Let's see the revelation.

> May God be gracious to us and bless us
> and make his face shine upon us,
> > Selah
> that your ways may be known on
> > earth,
> your salvation among all nations.
> May the peoples praise you, O God;
> may all the peoples praise you.
> May the nations be glad and sing for
> > joy,
> for you rule the peoples justly
> and guide the nations of the earth.
> > Selah
> May the peoples praise you, O God;
> may all the peoples praise you.
> Then the land will yield its harvest,
> and God, our God, will bless us.
> God will bless us,
> and all the ends of the earth will fear
> > him
> > > > Psalm 67:1-7

By this Psalm, God obviously said to David that salvation is for mankind. If it were not, he could never have written such a hymn song of vision of humanity. Then how can we know that this hymn is for mankind's salvation? We can say that based on these reasons.

First, salvation is universal. Let's see verse 2, "that your ways may be known on earth, your salvation among all nations." David proclaimed that the Lord's salvation was preached to all nations, to all the peoples.

Second, he proclaimed that all nations, all people, should praise God. Why should all people praise God? At first, they should praise God because of his salvation. All of God's people, who are saved by his grace, ought to praise God. Then they should praise God because of God's righteous judgment and rule. Finally, they should praise God because God has blessed his people.

Third, he proclaimed that all nations should fear God. Verse 7 says, "God will bless us, and all the ends of the earth will fear him." *Fear* means to revere and love God. We fear God because his holy character and judgment. But God gave grace to sinful men who deserved to be judged. By this reason all people should give thanks to God and love him. If we love him, we should obey him unconditionally.

Jesus Christ's Mission

God called Abraham for salvation of mankind and gave David the vision. Time passed; finally God's time of salvation had come. In other words, "The time had fully come" (Gal 4:4). The Bible says, "When the time had fully come, God sent his Son, born of a woman." What does this verse mean? Jesus Christ, God's Son, forsook heavenly glory and came as a human. In other words, he laid aside his divine power as God and made himself as a humble human being.

Without hesitation, Jesus became a man to dwell among the people and to save them from their sins. God called Abraham and revealed that he had a plan to send a Savior to the world through one of his descendants. Jesus Christ was the way of fulfillment of the promise of all nations' salvation that God showed David. Through him, not only will all people praise God, but also people will revere God. To fulfill the purpose, Jesus Christ was born of the Virgin Mary.

It is not easy to bring salvation to the whole world. So Jesus Christ chose the disciples and walked with them for 3 years. Finally, when Jesus gained the disciples' trust, He began to share his vision with them. As we know, the vision was to save all people, so Jesus planted the vision in his disciples. "Go into the world and preach the good news to all creation" (Mk 16:15); "Make disciples of all nations" (Mt 28:19);

"And repentance and forgiveness of sins will be preached …..to all nations" (Lk 24:47). "You will be my witnesses to the ends of the earth" (Acts 1:8).

Jesus fulfilled the final work of salvation for all people. He was crucified. He died for the redemption of all people from sin and judgment. He was indeed "the Lamb of God, who takes away the sin of the world" (Jn 1:29). He loved the World (Jn 3:16). His expression of love was to die for all people. Apostle John called Jesus' death: "He is the atoning sacrifice for our sins and not only for ours but also for the sins of the whole world" (1 Jn 2:2).

All people have sinned; therefore, they all die. No one can escape from death in the world. Everyone dies, regardless of whether he or she is poor or the rich, male or female, old or young, educated or uneducated. All die. We obviously know the fact that we are waiting for final judgment after death. This, short life and inescapable judgment could never be solved by sinful human beings. However Jesus Christ, our Savior solved the problem of death and judgment. How did he do that? He solved these problems as he died for man's sin on the cross and he was raised on the third day. Yes! Jesus Christ has risen and became a model for all believers. Whoever comes to Jesus Christ who died on the cross and was raised, repents of his sins, believes in Jesus and accepts him, they are saved.

My Mission

God was a God of mission at the time when he called Abraham, because God had the world in mind when he called Abraham. The God of mission gave David a vision of mission. The God of mission concretely presented the way for the salvation of the world. Beyond our expectation, the method was not good deeds, prayer, offering or help. Surprisingly, the method was that Christ Jesus, his one and only son came do bring it.

"An account of the genealogy of Jesus Christ the son of David, the son of Abraham," first verse of New Testament, teaches us three things.

First, Abraham lived like a missionary even though he was not a missionary; we have to live like that too. After all we are strangers and pilgrims. We do not put our heart- treasure in this world, but we have to live like a *missionary*.

What does it mean to live like a missionary? We have to reveal God directly or indirectly. Just as Abraham built an altar, we have to build an altar wherever we go and whatever we do. In other words we must worship God among the people. And we who live among unbelievers must pray for unbelievers' salvation. Not only that! We must testify to God's work in our lives whenever we have an opportunity.

Second, now we may not go to a foreign country like a missionary. However, we must have *a vision of mission* like David. In other words, we must bear the world in our heart. We should pray for the world to hear and respond to the gospel. We must pray for unbelievers' transformation, praise the Lord and fear God. Finally, we must believe that "this gospel of the kingdom will be preached in the whole world" (Mt 24:14).

The Bible reminds us, "Where there is no vision, the people perish" (Pro 29:18). Where there is no vision, the people perish. We must have a vision. What vision is it? Our vision means that our country needs to be saved, and reach the world from there. If we have a vision like this, then we will serve the God of mission.

Third, Jesus Christ died on the cross and was raised on the third day for world salvation. If we have a vision of the world mission, we must *preach,* "Be prepared in season and out of season," *Jesus Christ*, who is the way of salvation of the world. If we do not preach Jesus Christ, then who would save unbelievers? Undoubtedly other religions cannot save them. Many churches in Korea cannot save sinners either, because they don't have confidence in the gospel.

If we live a life of a missionary, like Abraham, and have a vision of mission like David, we can preach Jesus Christ who shouted, "It is finished" and died on the cross for the sins of the world. This is the good news of God's mission. We all must focus on mission in life, vision and preaching. If that is so, then we can say that we serve the God of mission.

Chapter 15

Faith, Hope, Love & Life

"An account of the genealogy of Jesus the Messiah, the son of David, the son of Abraham" (Matthew 1:1, NRSV).

This Sunday we celebrate the second worship service as well as the first communion service at this newly-built beautiful San Dol Church. As we take part in the sacrament, we are twice told of Jesus' admonition to "remember me" (1 Cor 11:24-25). We are also told of Paul's exhortation: "Whenever you eat this bread and drink this cup, you proclaim the Lord's death until he comes" (1 Cor 11:26).

When it comes to Jesus' admonition of "in remembrance of me," it carries three important meanings. First, remember the Lord of faith. All of us were sinners doomed to death and judgment. We were saved, however, through faith in Jesus Christ who shed his blood for us on the cross. Whenever we partake in the communion service, we should remember Jesus Christ, who is "the author and finisher of our faith" (Heb 12:2).

Second, remember the Lord of hope. The crucified Lord has risen and ascended! Someday he will come again to bring us believers into heaven free of pain and death, which is our ultimate hope. Whenever we take part in the communion service, we should remember Jesus Christ, who is "our hope" (1 Tim 1:1). As such, the communion service converges on Jesus Christ, who not only gives us faith and hope but also loves us.

Third, remember the Lord of love. Why did Jesus Christ die for us sinners at the hill of Calvary? Love! Unconditional love for us! In fact, we were sinners far from being worthy of God's redemptive love. Rather, God's punitive judgment was our inevitable destiny. God's agape, though, led Jesus Christ to be crucified so that we can have eternal life. Whenever we participate in the communion service, we should remember Jesus Christ, who is "love" (1 Jn 4:8).

Fourth, remember the Lord of Life. Jesus said, "I am the life..." (Jn 14:6). Jesus did all of these things and gave us all these provisions, so that we might have abundant life on earth and in heaven. In the provision of His Spirit, His kingdom will come, and His will can be done on earth, through his followers, as it is done in heaven. Whenever we participate in the communion service, we should remember Jesus Christ, who is "life."

The apostle Paul once proclaimed in 1 Corinthians 13:13: "And now these three remain: faith, hope and love. But the greatest of these is love." Why did he say such an expression? Because faith, hope and love are the heart and soul of the Christian life. We can find these three essentials in the communion service; in Paul's letters (Col 1:4-5; 1 Thes 1:3); and even in today's text, Matthew 1:1 reading, "An account of the genealogy of Jesus Christ the son of David, the son of Abraham."

Faith

Among the three figures mentioned in Matthew 1:1, who exemplified faith? Of course, Abraham did. Paul talked about him as follows: "Therefore, the promise comes by faith, so that it may be by grace and may be guaranteed to all Abraham's offspring—not only to those who are of the law, but also to those who are of the faith of Abraham. He is the father of us all" (Rom 4:16). To put it simply, Paul referred to Abraham as the father of our faith. Then, why did the apostle confer the glorious title upon Abraham? Because Abraham lived a life of faith by leaving, believing and giving.

To begin with, *by faith* Abraham "left, as the Lord had told him" (Gen 12:4) when "the LORD had said to him, 'Leave your country, your people and your father's household'" (Gen 12:1). Without faith, Abraham could not have obeyed God's command, because leaving his land meant the loss of a sense of security and leaving his family meant the loss of a sense of belonging. Abraham, though, stepped out of his comfort zone according to God's word "even though he did not know where he was going" (Heb 11:8), which was none other than a risk-taking faithful act.

In addition, *by faith* Abraham "believed God" (Gen 15:6) when God promised him a countless number of "descendents" with a "land" to inhabit (Gen 15: 5, 7). Without faith, Abraham could not have believed such a preposterous promise, because he was 75 years old with no children up to that moment. Abraham, though, held fast to the promise "even though he was past age—and Sarah herself was barren" (Heb 11:11), which was none other than a reason-defying faithful act.

Finally, *by faith* Abraham gave Isaac to God "as a burnt offering" (Gen. 22:3) when God ordered him to sacrifice the son. Of course, God saved Isaac's life at the last minute. Without faith, however, Abraham could not have offered up Isaac, because Isaac was a miracle child born to Abraham at the impossible age for fatherhood of 100 years old. Abraham, though, had no hesitation in sacrificing Isaac whom he loved more than his own life, which was none other than a self-denying faithful act.

Hope

It was David who embodied hope. Even though he was a man of faith and love, hope best characterized his life. Without hope, David might have faded into history as a faceless, nameless shepherd just like a countless number of other Israeli shepherds. Hope, though, made David totally different from them in attitude, behavior, and destiny. In particular, he got a grasp on hope at three crucial junctures on his life journey.

First of all, David lived *with hope* while he took care of his father's sheep. As the youngest son, David was by no means adored or acknowledged by his father, Jesse. To illustrate, Jesse invited every son at the feast for Samuel except for David, who was "tending the sheep" (1 Sam 16:11) as a forgotten son. David was also ridiculed and belittled by his elder brothers, which was well revealed in their attitude to him bringing the food for them in Saul's army: "Why have you come down here? And with whom did you leave those few sheep in the desert? I know how conceited you are and how wicked your heart is; you came down only to watch the battle" (1 Sam 17:28). In spite of it all, David put his hope in God alone, singing, "The LORD is my shepherd, I shall not be in want" (Ps 23:1). He was the very shepherd boy who *hopefully* praised even when the conditions may have justified complaint.

Not only that, David lived *with hope* after Samuel anointed him king. God chose David to be the second king of Israel, because he was "a man after His (God's) own heart" (1 Sam. 13:14). The stark reality was that David had to run away from Saul, the current king, who tried to kill him out of jealousy and hate. The hope that someday God would lift him up to the highest position in Israel, however, enabled David to persevere through all the hardships on the way to the throne. He was God's anointed who *hopefully* would endure even in the unbearable situation.

In the last analysis, David lived *with hope* when he ruled over Israel. The death of Saul was followed by David enthronement. He placed the kingdom on a solid base and desired in vain to construct a temple for

God. It was Solomon, not David, whom God selected to "build a house for me (God)" (1 Ch 17:12). Nevertheless, David gathered all the necessary materials for the construction of the Jerusalem Temple in the hope that his dream would come true through his offspring. He was the very king who *hopefully* prepared even in the hallowed position.

Love

Needless to say, Jesus Christ personified God's love on the face of the earth. He was the incarnation of *agape*—undeserved and unconditional love. If Jesus Christ had loved us with *stroge*—parental love, *phileo*—brotherly love, or *eros*—romantic love, no one would have been worthy of the love. The reason is simple! Each and every one of us was a wicked sinner totally unqualified to be God's child, Jesus' friend, or Christ's bride. Only because Jesus Chris loved us with agape could we be welcome, accepted, and forgiven. His agape was stronger than our sin!

The love of Jesus Christ was expressed and demonstrated in three dimensions. First, he has solved people's physical needs. During his public ministry Jesus Christ fed the hungry, healed the sick and diseased, cured the blind, deaf, lame, and dumb, drove demons out of the demon-possessed, and even raised the dead! All of these were an act of compassionate of his agape love.

Next, Jesus Christ has fulfilled humanity's spiritual needs. We human beings created in the image of God were alienated from the Creator because of sin. Without the occurrence of divine-human reconciliation, we cannot help but lead a hopeless life—living and dying in sin. By dying on the cross as a victory over sin, however, Jesus Christ reconciled us to God, thus meeting our deepest spiritual longings for salvation. In other words, we are forgiven, justified, and adopted into God's family thanks to Jesus' suffering and death by crucifixion, a sacrificial act springing from his agape love.

Last, Jesus Christ has satisfied believers' emotional needs. The moment we became children of God, the Holy Spirit entered into our heart, mind, and soul. Now the Holy Spirit dwells within us believers as our Comforter and Counselor. Walking with us every time and everywhere, the Holy Spirit gives us comfort, strength, and especially "my peace (the peace of Jesus Christ)" (Jn 14:27). Therefore, we can be peaceful under any circumstances—good or bad, rich or poor—enabled by *shalom* resulting from Jesus' agape love.

Life

As we now take part in the communion service, we should remember Jesus Christ and appreciate his giftive mission of faith, hope and love.[2] That is, he gave us enough faith to be saved from sin; he gave us joyful hope for the second-coming; above all, he gave us agape love on the cross. How thankful we should be to our Lord Jesus Christ, whose faith, hope and love have flowed into us abundantly, expectantly and unconditionally!

We have learned that today's text, Matthew 1:1, shows us faith, hope and love through three characters, Abraham, David and Jesus Christ, challenges us to follow in their footsteps and live a life of faith, hope and love. Our San Dol Church was built upon the faith in Jesus Christ. We are, thus, *a community of faith*. We must be united under one faith, Jesus Christ, and continue to share our faith with our neighbors in such a way that they can be invited into our faith community.

Our church is also *a community of love*. Our love toward one another made it possible for us to not only overcome our diverse backgrounds and characters but also commit ourselves to the construction of this beautiful sanctuary. We must keep on "fighting the good fight" (2 Tim 4:7), treating each other with agape love. If so, we will be recognized as true Christians by our Lord and the world, as Jesus Christ said, "By this all men will know that you are my disciples, if you love one another" (Jn 13:35).

Finally, our church is *a community of hope*. Our hope in Jesus Christ motivated us to start a church at home; to rent a middle school's classroom for worship services; at last to build this church building. In one sense, the new sanctuary in which we are now worshipping is God's gift resultant from our hope. We cannot stop here, though! We must move on with the blessed hope of parousia. Holding fast to the hope, we must proclaim Jesus Christ, the Lord of our faith; we must have agape love for each other; we must live a life of holiness, personally and socially. Then, to our neighbors who ask us for the reason for the faith, hope and love we have, we can give the joyful answer, "Jesus Christ is our life!"

---

[2] Giftive mission is a new missiological term based on the metaphor of God's free gift. Cf, Terry Muck & Frances Adeney, *Christianity Encountering World Religions* (Grand Rapids: Baker, 2009), 353-377.

www.ingramcontent.com/pod-product-compliance
Lightning Source LLC
Chambersburg PA
CBHW021812220426
43662CB00006B/290